GF01-BK

The University of Southern Mi

THE EFFECT OF WRITING AS EXPOSURE THERAPY

ON PTSD SYMPTOMS

by

Daniel Scott DeBrule

A Dissertation
Submitted to the Graduate Studies Office
of The University of Southern Mississippi
in Partial Fulfillment of the Requirements
for the Degree of Doctor of Philosophy

Approved:

_____
Director

_____

_____

_____

_____
University Director, Graduate Studies

August 2008

The University of Southern Mississippi

THE EFFECT OF WRITING AS EXPOSURE THERAPY

ON PTSD SYMPTOMS

by

Daniel Scott DeBrule

Abstract of a Dissertation
Submitted to the Graduate Studies Office
of The University of Southern Mississippi
in Partial Fulfillment of the Requirements
for the Degree of Doctor of Philosophy

August 2008

ABSTRACT

THE EFFECT OF WRITING AS EXPOSURE THERAPY ON PTSD SYMPTOMS

by Daniel Scott DeBrule

August 2008

The majority of empirically supported treatments for Posttraumatic Stress

Disorder involve some form of exposure, which desensitizes an individual to trauma-

related information. Theoretical work has suggested that the mechanism of exposure may

explain the tendency for writing to lessen symptoms, and empirical evidence of writing

and PTSD symptoms suggests that modifying the writing paradigm may result in better

symptom relief. The present investigation aimed to compare the efficacy of an exposure-

based writing intervention to the standard writing paradigm. A total of 68 undergraduates

that were screened for PTSD symptoms were randomly assigned to write about their most

severe trauma for 40 minutes, their most severe trauma for 20 minutes, or a control topic

for 20 minutes across four weekly writing sessions. The final sample included 48

participants who completed all four days of writing and the Posttraumatic Checklist-

Civilian Version, Impact of Events Scale – Revised, and Posttraumatic Dissociation Scale

at pretest and follow-up. Participants that wrote about trauma for 40 minutes were

expected to report less PTSD symptoms, dissociation, and health visits than participants

that write about trauma or a control topic for 20 minutes. No condition differences were

found. However, all participants improved on dependent measures regardless of writing

condition. Linguistic analysis of writing samples and essay ratings indicated that

participants generally followed directions, yet also suggested some possible design error for the present control topic. Analysis of continuous SUDS ratings, a unique aspect of the present study, indicated that writing for 40 minutes was associated with an initial increase then gradual decrease in anxiety. The present study was also unique in that all writing occurred within one year of Hurricane Katrina, which affected the present university and may have affected results. The present study is consistent with findings of other investigations of writing and PTSD that have found no effect, yet differ from a few investigations that have found an effect for PTSD symptoms, trauma reactivity, and depression. Future studies should consider implementing further design modifications to the writing paradigm in order to increase exposure to trauma and enhance effects for trauma-related outcomes.

ACKNOWLEDGEMENTS

The writer would like to thank Dr. Randolph Arnau and Dr. Lillian Range for their invaluable assistance and mentoring as directors of this project, as well as Dr. Brad Green, Dr. Mitchell Berman, Dr. William Lyddon, and Dr. Michael Madson for their insightful comments and suggestions as committee members. The writer would like to specifically recognize Dr. Lillian Range for sharing her extensive mentoring, invaluable advice, and expertise with writing research with the writer for the five years prior to being recognized as Professor Emeritus.

The writer would like to extend a very special thanks to Ginger Burge DeBrule for enormous support throughout this project. Appreciation must also be expressed to Deborah DeBrule, Scott DeBrule, and Wayne Yelton for their guidance, to Charles, David, John, Michael, Robert, and William Yelton for their encouragement, and to Ernest Sims and Kevin Smith for their camaraderie. The writer would also like to thank the participants in this project, who bravely wrote about very emotional, personal material while living in the aftermath of a severe hurricane.

TABLE OF CONTENTS

Clinical Presentation of PTSD
Treatment of PTSD
Writing Paradigm
Empirical evidence that writing can reduce PTSD symptoms

Participants
Measures
Procedure

Manipulation Check
Dependent Measures
SUDS Rating and Experiment Evaluation

Manipulation Check
Effect of Writing on PTSD Symptoms and Dissociation
Health Visits
Natural Disaster and the Writing Paradigm
Efficacy of Written Exposure

LIST OF TABLES

Table

LIST OF ILLUSTRATIONS

Figure

INTRODUCTION

Survivors of trauma often experience a myriad of negative consequences in their adjustment to traumatic stress, which can sometimes lead to Posttraumatic Stress Disorder (PTSD; American Psychiatric Association, 2000). Individuals meet criteria for PTSD when they experience symptoms of reexperiencing, avoidance, and hyperarousal for at least one month after sustaining a trauma that occurred at least four weeks ago (American Psychiatric Association, 2000). Although many survivors are able to return to their level of functioning prior to the trauma (Bonanno, 2004), a substantial percentage of survivors are unable to function in various life roles because of PTSD. Treatment of PTSD has primarily focused on exposing survivors to the emotional and cognitive upheaval of the trauma, which tends to neutralize PTSD symptoms by habituating individuals to maladaptive levels of arousal triggered by trauma-related stimuli (Foa & Kozak, 1986). Exposing individuals to their recollections of trauma or to trauma-related cues is arguably an essential component to any PTSD treatment.

An intervention involving expressive writing (Pennebaker, 2004) may serve as a means of exposure. This intervention, called the writing paradigm, involves writing about and fully describing the traumatic experience for 20 to 30 minutes (Richards, Beal, Seagal, & Pennebaker, 2000). Recent investigations have found that writing about trauma for three or four sessions lessened global PTSD symptoms, depression, and illness for trauma-exposed women (Sloan & Marx, 2004), when compared to their counterparts writing about trivial topics. Also, writing about the details of the traumatic experience has been utilized as a component of empirically validated PTSD treatments (Resick &

Schnicke, 1992a). However, few investigations have modified the writing paradigm to emulate design aspects of exposure therapy such as flooding (i.e., extending writing time to 45 minutes, Lango-Marsh & Spates, 2002) and so far, no study of the writing paradigm has screened individuals for PTSD as a criterion for inclusion in the study. Furthermore, few writing studies have evaluated several trauma related variables such as degree of exposure to trauma and trauma-related dissociation (Deters & Range, 2003). In fact, some have argued that the writing paradigm holds much heuristic value, suggesting that future investigations should utilize innovative design modifications to treat particularly difficult clinical presentations (King, 2004). The present investigation adapted the writing paradigm to emulate the flooding technique (Carroll & Foy, 1992) used in some exposure-based PTSD interventions; those who engage in four 40-minute sessions of writing about a trauma were expected to report less severe PTSD symptoms, trauma-related dissociation, and health visits than those who engaged in four 20-minute sessions of writing about a trauma or writing about a neutral topic as a control (the standard writing paradigm).

Clinical Presentation of Posttraumatic Stress Disorder

Approximately 25% of those who suffer a trauma develop PTSD (Davidson, Hughes, & Blazer, 1991). A trauma is operationalized by the Diagnostic and Statistical Manual of Mental Disorders – fourth edition (DSM-IV, American Psychiatric Association, 2000) as an event involving threat to one's physical safety or witnessing an event that endangered someone else's physical safety, to which the individual responded to with "intense fear, helplessness, or horror" (p. 467). Individuals that have suffered a trauma, which affects 40% of Americans before age 30 (Davidson, 1991), meet Criterion A for PTSD. Estimates of prevalence rates for PTSD among the US population range from approximately 10% (Davidson et al., 1991) to 8% (American Psychiatric Association, 2000). Certain risk factors predispose individuals to develop PTSD, such as experiencing childhood trauma, being a woman, experiencing sexual assault (Kessler, Sonnega, Bromet, & Nelson, 1995), and being exposed to a long-lasting trauma such as a natural disaster (McFarlane & Potts, 1997). The constellation of symptoms that characterize PTSD cluster into three distinct categories: Reexperiencing (Intrusion; Criterion B), Avoidance (Criterion C), and Hyperarousal (Criterion D; American Psychiatric Association, 2000). Also, dissociation is a symptom that is commonly comorbid with PTSD that can lead to severe impairment.

Intrusion entails a collection of five symptoms that involve the uncued reexperiencing of a trauma or reactivity to trauma-related stimuli. Individuals that endorse one of the following five symptoms meet Criterion B for PTSD: intrusive thoughts, nightmares, flashbacks, distress in response to trauma-related cues, and reactivity to trauma-related cues (American Psychiatric Association, 2000). An example of intrusion would be persistent fear-invoking nightmares and intrusive thoughts triggered by the smell of rain in a Vietnam combat veteran. Some forms of intrusion, such as nightmares, may be more prominent in women than men (Agargun, Kara, Ozer, Selvi, Kiran, & Ozer, 2003). Intrusion may initially lead individuals to fear encountering any trauma-related stimuli, which leads to symptoms of avoidance (Everly & Lating, 1995).

Avoidance entails the deliberate evading of any trauma-related information. Individuals that endorse three of the following seven symptoms meet Criterion C for PTSD: avoiding cognitions, emotions, or discussion related to trauma, avoiding locations and individuals that trigger recollections of trauma, being unable to recall a specific detail about the trauma, anhedonia, feeling detached or estranged, exhibiting a restricted affective range, and sensing that one will die at a young age (American Psychiatric Association, 2000). An example of avoidance would be emotional numbness and avoidance of rape-related information in women who suffer a sexual assault. Avoidance may be fairly resistant to pharmacological (Yehuda, Marshall, Penkower, & Wong, 2002) and psychological intervention (Foa & Meadows, 1997). Also, some have argued that avoidance may constitute two discrete constructs, emotional numbing/denial and deliberate avoidance of trauma-related stimuli (McDonald, 1997). Historically, PTSD was diagnosed when individuals met Criteria A, B, and C and exhibited impairment in daily functioning (American Psychiatric Association, 1994). However, the DSM-IV added a new symptom cluster to preexisting PTSD criteria: hyperarousal (American Psychiatric Association, 1994).

Hyperarousal entails five specific symptoms of PTSD. Individuals that endorse two of the following five symptoms meet Criterion D of the DSM-IV-TR: insomnia or hypersomnia, anger outbursts, concentration problems, paranoia, and startling excessively when hearing loud noises (American Psychiatric Association, 2000). A number of health-related problems have been identified that co-exist with hyperarousal, including hypertension, heart disease, ulcers, and irritable bowel syndrome (Everly & Lating,

1995). Also, high levels of hyperarousal predict worse PTSD symptom course and severity in a longitudinal trajectory analysis (Schell, Marshall, & Jaycox, 2004). The importance of hyperarousal as the most significant correlate of later PTSD symptoms suggests that interventions that target hyperarousal may reduce long-term incidence of and exacerbation of PTSD. Other writing paradigm studies have found that writing about trauma may lead to symptom improvement specifically for hyperarousal, rather than intrusion or avoidance (e.g., DeBrule & Range, 2005).

Dissociation that is related to trauma often occurs in trauma survivors. Although dissociation is a variable that should be consistently assessed in PTSD treatment (Carlson & Dutton, 2003), it is not required for a diagnosis of PTSD. Trauma-related dissociation can involve depersonalization, detachment from reality, and amnesia (Carlson & Waelde, 2000). Dissociation, particularly peritraumatic dissociation, has been identified as a strong risk factor for the development of PTSD (Marx & Sloan, 2005) Only one writing study has evaluated dissociation, and it found a decrease in dissociation from post-writing to follow-up for both the profound (trauma) and control condition, yet no significant change from prewriting to postwriting or from prewriting to follow-up (Deters & Range, 2003). However, this study utilized a measure of general dissociation rather than trauma-related dissociation. In contrast, the present study assessed dissociation that was specifically related to a trauma.

Individuals qualify for a PTSD diagnosis when they experience symptoms of intrusion, avoidance, and hyperarousal for one month or more, with an associated impairment in functioning. PTSD is also often associated with dissociation, which has been considered an important outcome measure in crime survivors (Carlson & Dutton, 2003). Clinicians may find that core PTSD symptoms, as well as common trauma-related symptoms such as dissociation (Everly & Lating, 2004), respond to treatments that involve exposure.

Treatment of PTSD

Treatments for PTSD are generally classified as psychosocial interventions (Foa & Meadows, 1997) or pharmacological interventions (Yehuda, et al., 2002), with some researchers advocating for a combination of psychosocial and pharmacological intervention (Shalev, Bonne, & Eth, 1996). Psychosocial interventions are subdivided into psychodynamic therapy (Lindy, Green, Grace, & Titchener, 1983), hypnotherapy (Brom, Kleber, & Defares, 1989), and cognitive-behavioral treatments, which, unlike psychodynamic or hypnotic approaches, are empirically supported by a wealth of treatment outcome studies with high integrity (Foa & Meadows, 1997). Cognitive-behavioral treatments for PTSD include imaginal flooding (Cooper & Clum, 1989), implosive flooding (Keane, Fairbank, Caddell, & Zimering, 1989), prolonged exposure (Foa, Rothbaum, Riggs, & Murdoch, 1991), stress inoculation training, (Kilpatrick, Veronen, & Resick, 1982), and cognitive processing therapy (Resick & Schnicke, 1992a). Although a thorough review of the existing cognitive behavioral PTSD treatments is beyond the scope of the present investigation (See Meadows & Foa, 1998; Rothbaum, Meadows, Resick, 2000, for review), exposure therapy has yielded superior findings to other treatments (Astin & Rothbaum, 2000).

Exposure therapy reduces PTSD symptoms in trauma survivors. A recent review revealed that 11 of 12 investigations that utilize exposure led to significant symptom reduction, with the only exception not leading to change because combat veterans were exposed to shame and guilt-related stimuli, rather than anxiety-provoking stimuli (Astin & Rothbaum, 2000). Exposure has also been empirically proven in terms of its use across trauma populations, and tends to lead to more rapid improvement than any other existing PTSD treatment regardless of the type of trauma (Astin & Rothbaum, 2000). In exposure therapy, trauma survivors describe their trauma using the present tense for approximately one hour and "use as much detail as possible, especially sensory memories such as smells, sounds, etc., as well as thoughts and feelings experienced during the event" (Astin & Rothbaum, 2000, p. 51). Thus, writing studies seeking to mimic exposure protocols should involve individuals writing for longer than 20 minutes about the sensory details of trauma, in addition to thoughts and feelings. Two forms of exposure are particularly relevant to writing investigations: Cognitive Processing Therapy and flooding.

Writing has been utilized in Cognitive Processing Therapy (CPT; Resick & Schnicke, 1992a) as a means of exposure. In CPT, survivors "write an account of the rape...all of the sensory details, emotions, and thoughts they could remember (Resick & Schnicke, p. 751, 1992b)." They write and then read their writing sample for approximately 90-minutes for session three and four in a 12-session protocol. The therapist encourages the client to process their emotional reaction as they write. CPT is an empirically validated treatment for PTSD and has yielded treatment gain results similar to prolonged exposure (Resick, Nishith, Weaver, Astin, & Feuer, 2002).

Writing may also be utilized as a form of flooding, which typically exposes an individual to the sensory details, thoughts, and emotions experienced briefly before trauma, during trauma, and briefly after trauma (Carroll & Foy, 1992). The flooding procedure typically involves a secure environment, SUDS ratings, selection of one trauma to be disclosed, and development of a "scene" lasting 15 to 20 minutes that details the trauma (Carroll & Foy, 1992). Sessions are typically designed with two 20-minute exposures to a specific trauma separated by a five-minute break (Carroll & Foy, 1992, p. 58). Therefore, the current study, which includes a condition designed to emulate flooding exposure, utilized a similar protocol that asked participants to write about their trauma for 40 total minutes. They were also be asked to provide as many sensory details related to a specific trauma throughout writing.

Exposure therapy has proven to be an empirically supported treatment for PTSD symptoms (Astin & Rothbaum, 2000). Writing appears to reduce symptoms because of the mechanism of exposure, in that individuals habituate to trauma-related stimuli through written disclosure (Sloan & Marx, 2004). Writing is also utilized in an empirically-supported PTSD treatment, CPT, as the exclusive means of exposure during two lengthy writing sessions and rereading of the written account. Finally, the parameters for the flooding protocol may be easily reconciled with the standard writing paradigm by extending writing time and requesting sensory details during writing. The present study seeks to compare the efficacy of such an exposure-based writing intervention with the standard writing paradigm.

The Writing Paradigm

A writing paradigm developed by James Pennebaker (Pennebaker & Beall, 1986) typically involves random assignment of participants to one of two or more conditions: an experimental (also called profound) condition where participants write about a disturbing, emotional topic or a control (also called trivial) condition where participants write about a neutral, innocuous topic. Participants in both conditions typically write for a time period ranging from 15 to 30 minutes and for three or four sessions. This writing often occurs in successive days (e.g., Scott, Harrington, House, & Ferrier, 1999) or may occur over a longer period of time, such as two weeks (e.g., Kovac & Range, 1999). Participants complete questionnaires before writing, directly after writing, and weeks after writing has taken place, yet often measures have also been given months after the writing occurs (Francis & Pennebaker, 1992).

Self-help protocols for the writing paradigm exist in which the individual can personalize a writing intervention (Pennebaker, 2004). The development of this paradigm has spurred a great deal of interest in the benefits of writing process, yet few writing paradigm studies have investigated PTSD symptoms in a trauma-exposed sample.

Writing has often, but not always, been found to be beneficial. In a meta-analysis of 13 studies using the writing paradigm, the overall effect of written disclosure ($d = .47$) was statistically significant across all 13 studies (Smyth, 1998). People randomly assigned to an experimental writing condition improved by 23% over those randomly assigned to the trivial condition (Smyth, 1998). This amount of improvement indicates that writing about a traumatic or stressful event typically causes an improvement of almost half a standard deviation for the dependent variable of interest.

In this meta-analysis, dependent measures were categorized as reported health, psychological well-being, physiological functioning, general functioning, and health behaviors. All categories improved except for health behaviors. Psychological and physiological well-being improved most. Men benefited significantly more than women from writing, perhaps because men in general engage in less emotional disclosure. Published and unpublished studies were not significantly different in effect size, nor were studies in which participants wrote about a far removed or more recent trauma. Moreover, the number of writing sessions had no statistically significant effect, but studies with relatively longer writing periods (e.g., 30 minutes compared to 15 minutes; Smyth, 1998) exhibited stronger effect sizes. However, no writing study in the meta-analysis reported a writing time equivalent to the time associated with empirically supported forms of exposure (Resick & Schnicke, 1992b), although meta-analysis has suggested that longer writing times may enhance effect. Thus, in the present investigation, the amount of time during and between sessions will be lengthened and measures of psychological well-being and physical health will be analyzed for gender differences.

Writing in experimental designs has lead to promising benefits that suggest PTSD could be affected. Writing has yielded a positive effect for general dependent measures of physical health, psychological health, and cognitive health.

Physical health has been found to improve after writing about a trauma. For example, individuals who wrote about a stressful topic were found to have increased levels of immunological markers CD3, CD4, CD8, and CD16 (Petrie, Booth, &

Pennebaker, 1998) compared to individuals who wrote about trivial topics. This finding

was replicated by a study that found that those who wrote about stress were found to have

improved immunity compared to those who wrote about a trivial topic, with women

exhibiting significantly higher CD4 levels than men (Petrie, Booth, & Pennebaker, 1998)

In a similar study, those who wrote about illness were found to have a significant increase

in pulmonary expiratory volume in asthma patients and decreased disease activity in

arthritis patients (Smyth et al., 2000) compared to those who wrote about a trivial topic.

In addition to specific physiological measures, health visits or doctor visits have

provided a measure of physical health in writing paradigm studies. Health visits have

been found to decrease among college students who wrote about a stressful or traumatic

experience (Greenberg & Stone, 1992; Pennebaker & Francis, 1996) compared to

students who wrote about a control topic. Also, health visits decreased for trauma writers

in a prison population compared to control writers (Richards et al., 2000). However,

health visits did not decrease for those who wrote about sudden bereavement (Range,

Kovac, & Marion, 2000) or the suicide of a loved one (Kovac & Range, 2000). The

inconsistency of the effect of writing on health visits may occasionally be attributable to

all conditions exhibiting a decrease in health visits (i.e., Deters & Range, 2003). In other

words, in some studies, health visits decreased for all writer, regardless of whether they

wrote about a profound or trivial topic. Although the effect of writing on health visits has

been inconsistent, the outcome is often assessed with only one subjective question.

Number of health visits, which is an indication of physical health, will constitute a dependent measure in the present study.

Psychological health generally improves after writing about a trauma, with some exceptions. Negative psychological constructs such as grief, suicide, depression, and PTSD symptoms have been assessed in recent writing paradigm studies more frequently, whereas most of the initial writing paradigm investigations assessed health-related constructs. Grief over a suicide reduced in those who wrote about bereavement, yet overall grief did not change (Kovac & Range, 2000), which is consistent with other studies (Range et al., 2000). Suicidality did not change after writing (Kovac & Range, 2000). The effect of writing on depression has varied, as some investigations have found benefits (Lepore, 1997; Sloan & Marx, 2004) and some studies have found no change after writing (Donnelly & Murray, 1991; Kloss & Lisman, 2002). Intrusion and avoidance have been lessened exclusively in trauma conditions (Lepore, 1997), as well as both trauma and control conditions (Deters & Range, 2003). Thus, psychological constructs such as intrusion, avoidance, and depression tend to respond to the writing paradigm, whereas grief and suicidality do not respond.

Positive psychological constructs have been investigated as well. Journaling enhances optimism (Mann, 2001) and posttraumatic growth when assessed directly after writing (Ullrich & Lutgendorf, 2002). The writing paradigm resulted in no significant change in posttraumatic growth directly after writing or at follow-up (DeBrule & Range, 2005). Overall, negative psychological constructs tend to improve after the writing paradigm is implemented, whereas positive psychological constructs have yielded mixed results.

Cognitive health has improved in some writing paradigm studies. Grade point average (GPA) increased for those who wrote about a stressful topic compared to those who wrote about a neutral topic (Klein & Boals, 2001). Working memory, defined as the ability to simultaneously attend to and process incoming stimuli, increased after trauma writing but not for neutral writing. Findings suggest that the increase in working memory resulted in the increase in GPA, due to students gaining a better ability to retain information and follow complex directions (Klein & Boals, 2001). Furthermore, several writing investigations have examined the frequency of cognitive words used in each essay, generally finding that experimental groups use significantly more than control groups (DeBrule & Range, 2005; Deters & Range, 2003). In the present investigation, linguistic analysis of three cognitive word counts (cognitive mechanism, insight, and causal) will be utilized as a manipulation check to ensure that trauma writers actually write about a trauma.

Writing paradigm studies have focused mostly on physical, psychological, and cognitive aspects of well-being. Also, PTSD symptoms would appear to be responsive to the writing paradigm, given that the paradigm reduced depression and intrusion. However, a small number of writing paradigm studies have involved trauma survivors and/or measures of common responses to trauma, such as PTSD and dissociation, compared to the large number of writing studies that have assessed more general measures of physical and psychological health.

Theoretical evidence writing and PTSD

There are both theoretical and empirical reasons why writing has been proposed as a means of decreasing PTSD symptoms. One predominant theory that is widely cited for the etiology of PTSD as well as other anxiety disorders, such as phobias, is Mowrer's two-factor theory (Mowrer, 1960). The first factor of Mowrer's theory suggests that PTSD initially begins when individuals experience heightened anxiety during a trauma, and become classically conditioned to experience anxiety when they confront trauma-related stimuli (Kring, Davison, Neale, & Johnson, 2007). The second factor suggests that PTSD is maintained by operant conditioning, specifically negative reinforcement, when trauma survivors avoid trauma-related stimuli and associated anxiety, thereby strengthening the anxiety response (Kring et al., 2007). Theoretically, writing may provide a means of exposure to trauma-related stimuli, which in turn should reduce related anxiety and avoidance through habituation. Also, initial empirical evidence of improvement in symptoms of depression (Lepore, 1997) and general health (Richards et al., 2000) have led to an emerging interest in the effect of writing among trauma survivors who are currently distressed.

Writing about a trauma constitutes a form of exposure, which theoretically should habituate trauma writers to trauma-related information. Some have argued that exposure is the essential ingredient in any successful treatment for PTSD (Foa & Kozak, 1986), as exposure should typically trigger reactivity in clients who then experience habituation to fear associated with trauma-related information. Although uncontrolled expression of emotion can be unproductive and harmful, structured expression of emotion appears to be therapeutic (Littrell, 1999). Writing provides a format for the controlled, structured expression of emotion. In fact, writers who compose cohesive stories of trauma exhibit more benefits than writers who simply list aspects of trauma (Smyth, True, & Souto, 2001). Finally, others posit that writing constitutes exposure when writers only discuss one trauma, habituate to negative affect experienced initially during writing, and write across numerous sessions for maximum habituation (Sloan, Marx & Epstein, 2005). Thus, writing about a trauma may reduce PTSD symptoms by providing a structured means of disclosing emotionally painful memories, which trauma writers habituate to over time, prompting symptom improvement.

Empirical evidence has suggested that writing can be a means of reducing intrusion. Studies that evaluated the effect of writing and emotional expression consistently found that individuals who inhibited the expression of negative emotion reported significantly more internal distress, reportedly caused by unyielding rumination. Therefore, the benefits of writing may be due to writing providing a release for negative thoughts and feelings, which leads to a reduction in unwanted, intrusive thinking (Pennebaker, 1989). Trauma commonly results in rumination, or intrusive thought (Creamer, Burgess, & Pattison, 1992), which can reinforce negative emotion if left unchecked (Nolen-Hoeksema & Morrow, 1991). Writing about stressful topics can reduce negative, intrusive thinking as well (Lepore, 1997). Therefore, both theoretical and empirical support exists for the potential of writing to reduce intrusion.

Writing investigations have been conducted with trauma survivors and trauma related variables other than PTSD symptoms, such as depression and anxiety. One of the first writing paradigm investigations involving trauma survivors investigated the effects on health measures, finding that writing about an imaginary or a real trauma led to fewer health visits, than writing about a control topic (Greenberg, Wortman, & Stone, 1996). Another writing paradigm investigation found that participants in a trauma writing condition, control writing condition, and an innovative positive writing condition did not differ on self-reported depression, anxiety, or physical health, yet only 9% of the trauma writers actually wrote about a trauma (Kloss & Lisman, 2002). Thus, there was a manipulation error such that most participants in the trauma condition did not follow protocol, suggesting that dependent measures did not respond to experimental writing because there was no experimental condition. Overall, writing has reduced symptoms of depression, generalized anxiety and physical health in trauma survivors, yet few investigations have evaluated PTSD symptoms.

Theoretical and empirical evidence suggests that writing holds much promise in the context of PTSD. Writing may serve as an exposure tool, yet the four 20-minute writing sessions associated with the writing paradigm may not lead to adequate exposure or the resulting habituation that is typically a component of empirically supported PTSD treatments. Initial empirical evidence for writing to reduce intrusion (Lepore, 1997) and hyperarousal (DeBrule & Range, 2005) suggests that writing may be practical and effective for to trauma survivors, who have seldom been involved in writing investigations. Studies that have examined writing and trauma survivors often assess variables such as depression, anxiety, and health. Although there is a dearth of writing investigations among survivors with PTSD symptoms, a few investigations have evaluated the specific effects of the standard writing paradigm or similar writing protocols on PTSD symptoms.

Empirical evidence that writing can reduce PTSD symptoms

Few investigations have evaluated the effect of writing on trauma survivors. These investigations have tended to yield a positive effect, although a few have failed to significantly change PTSD symptoms. To date, there have been eight investigations of writing interventions that have specifically assessed PTSD symptoms in trauma survivors: three that adhere to the writing paradigm, and five that represent a variation on the original paradigm.

The first writing paradigm investigation that focused primarily on PTSD symptoms also evaluated other trauma-related constructs, such as general dissociation, depression, and suicidality (Deters & Range, 2003). Undergraduate women and men ($N =$ 57) who were screened for trauma wrote four times for 15 minutes about either their deepest trauma-related feelings and emotions or a control topic. Trauma writers reported a decrease in PTSD symptoms, depression, suicidality, and dissociation from prewriting to six-week follow-up, yet control writers reported similar improvement in all of their symptoms as well, and maintained this improvement at follow-up (Deters & Range, 2003). The present investigation will build upon this study by assessing trauma-related dissociation rather than general dissociation.

A second writing paradigm study evaluated PTSD symptoms, depression, physical health, and cortisol (Sloan & Marx, 2004). Undergraduate women who were screened for trauma ($N = 49$) wrote three times for 20 minutes about either their deepest feelings and emotions relative to trauma or about a control topic. Decreases in PTSD symptoms ($r_{effect\,size} = .43$) and physical health ($r_{effect\,size} = .49$) achieved statistical significance for trauma writers compared to control writers, yet did not achieve clinical significance. Depression ($r_{effect\ size}$ = .72) also improved for trauma writers compared to control writers, and clinical significance was indicated by Reliable Change Index (RCI = 2.54, p < .05). Furthermore, reactivity to trauma-related information, as measured by comparing Day 1 prewriting cortisol levels to postwriting cortisol levels, was associated with outcome measure change scores in PTSD symptoms and depression. This finding suggests that writing did yield significant habituation to the trauma based on postwriting cortisol measurements taken directly after participants recorded a spoken description of the trauma. Design characteristics such as testing for clinical significance and assessing trauma-related physiological variables, such as cortisol, is recommended for future investigations (Sloan & Marx, 2004). The present investigation will assess reactivity to written exposure through use of SUDS throughout the writing task.

A third writing paradigm study evaluated PTSD symptoms and posttraumatic growth (DeBrule & Range, 2005). Undergraduate women and men who were screened for trauma (N = 51) wrote four times for 20 minutes about either their deepest feelings and emotions related to the most severe trauma or a control topic. Hyperarousal improved for trauma writers compared to control writers (η^2 = .20), yet participants in both conditions reported improvement in global PTSD symptoms and intrusion based on Impact of Events Scale (Weiss & Marmar, 1996) scores at follow-up. Posttraumatic growth and avoidance did not change for trauma writers or control writers. Writing may affect hyperarousal by fostering better physiological regulation, and allowing for the disinhibition of trauma-related information (DeBrule & Range, 2005). The present investigation will strengthen the writing intervention so that intrusion and avoidance might be expected to respond in addition to hyperarousal.

The first modified writing investigation evaluated PTSD symptoms in a Middle Eastern hospital (Gidron, Peri, Connolly, & Shalev, 1996). Trauma survivors who were being treated for PTSD ($N = 14$) wrote about their trauma or a control topic. Trauma writers then read their writing to the group. Unexpectedly, writing exacerbated PTSD symptoms. However, the small sample size and possible confounding variables (i.e., psychotropic medication and the instructions to read their writing to a group) limit the usefulness and interpretability of these findings. The present investigation will exclude individuals who are receiving pharmacological or psychological treatment for PTSD.

The second modified writing investigation evaluated PTSD symptoms as well as social anxiety and depression (Brown & Heimberg, 2001). Undergraduate women ($N = 77$) participated in one of four conditions in a 2 X 2 design: writing facts about the trauma once versus writing facts and emotions about the trauma once, then reading their written account to themselves versus reading their written account to a confederate. PTSD symptoms, depression, and social avoidance did not change regardless of writing task or verbal disclosure method from prewriting to a one-month follow-up. However, change scores in depression and social avoidance correlated with greater detail in linguistic analysis, suggesting that writers should be encouraged to focus on the details of their trauma (Brown & Heimberg, 2001). In the present investigation, the exposure condition was instructed to focus on the sensory details of trauma.

A third modified writing investigation evaluated PTSD symptoms as well as depression (Barry & Singer, 2001). Mothers ($N = 62$) who had an infant placed in the Neonatal Intensive Care Unit either journalled about their experience for at least 30 minutes on four consecutive days or were placed on a waiting list. Global PTSD symptoms, as well as intrusion, avoidance, and hyperarousal, significantly improved among journaling mothers compared to non-journaling mothers. Also, four initially depressed women in the journaling group reported no depression at follow-up, yet no women in the wait-listed control group reported such improvement. Hyperarousal (Cohen's $d = 1.02$) exhibited the highest effect size, and global PTSD symptoms ($d = .77$), intrusion ($d = .62$), and avoidance ($d = .53$) exhibited a moderate effect, suggesting that writing may affect hyperarousal more than other symptom clusters.

A fourth modified writing investigation evaluated PTSD symptoms, anxiety, hypnotizability, and treatment expectancy (Lango-Marsh & Spates, 2002). Community women and men who met full or partial criteria for PTSD ($N = 24$) wrote for approximately 60 minutes or engaged in Eye Movement Desensitization Reprocessing (EMD/R) for at least three sessions, with fewer sessions occurring if SUDS or Validity of Cognition Scale scores became asymptotic, which was rare. Writers were instructed to focus on emotions, cognitions, and sensory details relative to trauma. Both writers and EMD/R participants reported a decrease in symptoms of intrusion, avoidance, and generalized anxiety from pre-to post, and maintained this improvement at a 1-2 week follow-up. Client expectancy and hypnotizability did not account for treatment gains. Modifying writing instructions to mirror preexisting protocols for PTSD appear to reduce intrusion and avoidance (Lango-Marsh & Spates, 2002), and the standard writing paradigm reduces hyperarousal (DeBrule & Range, 2005), yet the effect of modified writing on hyperarousal is yet unclear. The present investigation will extend the writing time in an effort to increase the effect of writing as an exposure tool.

A fifth modified writing investigation evaluated PTSD symptoms, anxiety, depressive symptoms, and mood (Schoutrop, Lange, Hanewald, Davidovich, & Salomon, 2002). Undergraduate women and men ($N = 48$) either wrote about trauma five times for 45 minutes across two weeks or were placed on a waiting list. Intrusion, avoidance, and depressive symptoms improved for writers compared to non-writers, yet anxiety and mood did not differ between groups. Secondary variables such as somatization, hostility, and sleeping problems also did not differ between groups. Thus, this study provided evidence that increasing the number of writing sessions and writing time is associated with reduce intrusion and avoidance associated with a trauma (Scoutrop et al., 2002). Therefore, the present investigation will extend the writing time from 20 minutes, which typically occurs in the writing paradigm, to 40 minutes, similar to exposure protocols.

Writing has led to improved PTSD symptoms in terms of global symptoms, intrusion, avoidance, and/or hyperarousal in a majority of investigations that have either adhered to or modified the writing paradigm. Investigations that have failed to find improvement of PTSD symptoms after writing may have clouded possible treatment gains because of limitations such as inaccurate screening (Deters & Range, 2003) and instructing participants to read writing samples to themselves (Brown & Heimberg, 2001) or others (Gidron et al., 1996). Several studies that have examined change in PTSD symptoms at postwriting have tended to find no improvement (DeBrule & Range, 2005) or exacerbations (Deters & Range, 2003). Also, PTSD symptoms appear to respond better to writing interventions with longer writing time and/or number of sessions. More specifically, interventions that request great detail about the emotional, cognitive, *and* sensory reactions to trauma (Brown & Heimberg, 2001; Lango-Marsh & Spates, 2002) and mirror preexisting forms of exposure (Lango-Marsh & Spates, 2002; Scoutrop et al., 2002) appear to reduce PTSD symptoms more than standard writing paradigm interventions.

The present investigation will integrate several design alterations that have been suggested by recent writing studies. One, writing instructions will request that trauma writers describe the sensory details that are associated with the trauma. Two, the writing paradigm will be extended from the four standard 20-minute writing sessions that occur within days to four 40-minute writing sessions that occur weekly . Three, in addition to PTSD symptoms, the present investigation will assess trauma-related dissociation, general health, and trauma related variables such as exposure and amount of threat to physical integrity as dependent variables. Four, writing sessions will be structured to mimic pre-existing exposure protocols. Five, SUDS will be assessed throughout writing, in order to correlate symptom change with the degree to which participants emotionally react to the writing sessions. Six, the screening procedure (Carlson & Dutton, 2003) will assess the experience of a DSM-IV Criterion A trauma and PTSD symptoms by utilizing a diagnostically sensitive self-report measure. Seven, no posttest measure will be utilized due to several writing studies finding no symptom change (DeBrule & Range, 2005) or exacerbated symptoms (Deters & Range, 2003) briefly after writing, which may be a result of the short-term increase in negative mood and anxiety often associated with writing about trauma. The primary hypothesis of the present investigation is that screened undergraduates that engage in exposure-based writing will report a decrease in PTSD symptoms, trauma-related dissociation, and illness from prewriting to follow-up, and that the decrease will be greater than that experienced by those who engage in writing paradigm through trauma or control writing.

METHOD

Participants

A power analysis was conducted in order to calculate how many participants to include in the present study. The overall effect size that was found in a recent meta-analysis (Smyth, 1998) for writing paradigms ($d = .47$) was utilized. The power analysis, using Cohen's suggestion that power should equal .8, and alpha should equal .05, indicated that the total sample size needed for these parameters is 74. Thus, all three conditions will need to contain at least 25 participants in order to provide appropriate power. Given an approximate 20% rate of attrition in writing paradigm studies (Kovac & Range, 2000), a total of 90 was selected as the target number for participants. However, due to numerous circumstances that emerged during the study (logistical problems related to Hurricane Katrina, phone/email contacts inoperable, many declined participation), a total of 68 participants were asked to complete all phases of the present study across three semesters.

All participants were chosen from a screening process, which included a brief screen for exposure to traumatic event(s) (Carlson & Dutton, 2004), and the Screen for Posttraumatic Stress Symptoms (SPTSS; Carlson, 2001). Respondents were eligible for participation if they reported experiencing a trauma that occurred at least two months ago that involved a threat of death, triggered an extreme negative reaction, and resulted in significant PTSD symptoms. Respondents who suffered a trauma within two months were excluded, since they could be suffering from Acute Stress Disorder, rather than PTSD.

A total of 796 screening forms (See Appendix A) were distributed to several undergraduate classes, and were used to select students that met criteria for inclusion. Of the 796 that were screened, 176 were excluded because they declined participation on the screening form by responding "no" to a question regarding interest in a study about writing and trauma. This was an exceptionally high rate compared to other studies at the present university that reported fewer than 20 of 711 students screened declined participation (DeBrule & Range, 2005). Of the 620 that remained, 289 listed an event that was not consistent with a DSM-IV Criterion A trauma. Of the 331 that remained, 212 did not endorse resulting symptoms of a severe enough degree to be consistent with PTSD on the SPTSS. Therefore, the screening process yielded a total of 119 undergraduates who were suffering from significant PTSD symptoms following a trauma were contacted for potential participation. Of the 119 that were contacted, a total of 68 participants began the study after scheduling a time with the primary investigator and keeping their appointment.

Of the 68 participants who completed prewriting measures and at least one day of writing, 50 were women (73.5%) and 18 were men who ranged in age from 18 to 57, with a mean age of 21.71 ($SD = 5.72$). In terms of ethnicity, 40 identified themselves as Caucasian (58.8%), 25 identified themselves as African-American (36.8%), and the final three participants identified themselves as Hispanic American, Asian American, or Other. Participants represented educational class somewhat equally, with 16 seniors (23.5%), 13 juniors (19.1%), 13 sophomores (19.1%), and 26 freshman (38.2%) participating in Day 1 of the study.

Participants were given free-response area to report their most severe trauma, as well as any secondary traumas that they had experienced. The most severe traumas represented eight categories: 11 (16.2%) reported a physical assault, 11 (16.2%) reported a traumatic bereavement, 8 (11.8%) reported a natural disaster, 7 (10.3%) reported a sexual assault or rape, 6 (8.8%) reported abuse, 6 (8.8%) reported a motor vehicle accident involving severe injury or threat to life, 5 (7.4%) reported a general life-threatening trauma (e.g., nearly drowned), and 4 (5.9%) reported combat in Iraq or Afghanistan. The remaining ten participants (14.7%) reported an experience that did not meet the DSM-IV definition of a trauma, such as bereavement, parental divorce, or illness of a family member. Of these 10 participants, eight participants reported a secondary trauma that was consistent with DSM-IV criteria.

For the question regarding secondary trauma(s), 48 participants identified a trauma consistent with DSM-IV criteria, 13 identified a non-traumatic event, and 7 did not respond. Hurricane Katrina was identified by seven participants as their most severe trauma and by nine participants as a secondary trauma.

Participants also reported various aspects of their most severe traumatic experience, including the time since the trauma occurred, the length of the trauma, and the extent of danger involved. Participants reported an average of 1963.08 days since the trauma occurred ($SD = 2630.27$), with a range from 61 to 18,519 days. Approximately half (45%) of the participants reported that their most severe trauma occurred three years or less, with 19% reporting that the trauma occurred within the past year. Participants varied widely with regard to the duration of their trauma ($M = 248.05$ days, $SD = 599.53$), with 11 (16.2%) reporting seconds to several minutes, 39 (57.4%) reporting one day to a month, 9 (13.2%) reporting one month to a year, and 9 (13.2%) reporting over one year. Many participants reported that their trauma involved a very low or very high threat of danger, as 15 (22.1%) ranked danger as a 1 while 17 (25%) ranked danger as a 10. Most participants (61.8%) reported danger as a 6 or above ($M = 6.04$). Overall, the participants who began the study represented a diversity of trauma exposure that varied in terms of duration, danger, and time since the experience.

Of the 68 participants who began the study, many were lost to attrition. Ten participants failed to return after Day 1, two failed to return after Day 2, and one failed to return after Day 3. Seven participants completed all four days of writing, but failed to complete follow-up measures. Thus, a total of 20 participants were lost to attrition. The present study examined 48 participants who completed all four days of writing and follow-up measures.

The final sample of 48 participants included 37 women (77%) and 11 men. Regarding ethnicity, 27 participants identified themselves as Caucasian (58%), 18 as African-American (35%), 1 as Asian-American, 1 as Hispanic, and 1 as Other. The final sample was heterogeneous in terms of educational class, with 13 seniors (27%), 11 juniors (23%), 9 sophomores (19%), and 15 freshman (32%) being represented. The final sample was very similar to the starting sample with regard to the traumas experienced, time since the trauma, danger involved, and duration of the experience. Several one-way ANOVAs (Group: Completed vs. Attrition) indicated that participants who did not complete the study were not significantly different from those who did complete in terms of demographics, trauma-related variables, or pretest dependent measures.

Measures

A *Screening Form* (See Appendix A) adapted from DSM-IV criteria for a traumatic experience (American Psychiatric Association, 2000) was used to determine if potential participants met criteria for inclusion in the study. The first question of the form asked students if they had endured a traumatic experience by asking students to check yes or no boxes for different common forms of trauma (vehicle wreck or accident, natural disaster, physical assault or abuse, sexual assault or abuse, being attacked, dangerous military combat, sudden bereavement, witnessing a death or severe injury, or any event involving significant fear). Next, respondents indicated if any of the traumas they had experienced bothered them emotionally. If they answered yes to this question, respondents then responded to nine questions that provided further information about each event.

Respondents were then asked to (a) indicate the letter that corresponds to a traumatic event listed above; (b) indicate their age at the time of trauma; (c) describe the event in a free-response area; (d) answer two yes/no questions that asked respondents if the event involved death or injury or fear of death or injury; (e) answer two yes/no questions that asked if respondents felt "very afraid, helpless, or horrified" or "unreal, spaced out, disoriented, or strange (Carlson, 2001)" during the trauma; and (f) indicate the amount of time that passed before respondents were bothered by the event, then indicate the extent of their emotional distress on a 5-point Likert scale (Carlson, 2001; See Appendix A).

A brief *Contact Questionnaire* (Appendix B) asked participants to indicate if they were interested in a research study involving trauma. Those who were interested provided three forms of contact (Home phone number, cellular phone number, and email address) and indicated their preferred means of contact. They were then asked to identify their most severe trauma and report how long ago it occurred. Finally, participants were asked if they were seeking treatment or using medication for any mental illness at the present time.

The *Screen for Posttraumatic Stress Symptoms* (SPTSS; Carlson, 2001) consists of 17 items that gauge common PTSD symptoms (e.g., "I have trouble getting to sleep or staying asleep.") that are scored depending on symptom frequency during the past two weeks (from 0 = "if you never had the experience" to 10 = "if it was always happening to you or happened every day"). Higher scores indicate more severe symptoms, with a range from 0 to 170. The SPTSS was designed as a PTSD screen that provides a very brief (three to five minutes) and readable (Flesch grade level of 7.5) alternative to more lengthy screens that are difficult to read. In addition to a total scores, the SPTSS yields scores for three subscales that assess the three symptom clusters of PTSD: Intrusion, avoidance, and hyperarousal. The SPTSS was utilized in the present investigation as a screen for mild to moderate PTSD symptoms (Carlson, 2001; See Appendix C). Respondents met inclusion for the present study if they reported a mean score of 4.0 and higher on the SPTSS, which results in sensitivity of .94 for PTSD (Carlson, 2001).

The SPTSS has exhibited internal consistency, and significant item-total correlations among 136 psychiatric inpatients. Cronbach's alpha was .91 for the global scale. Item-total correlations were noteworthy for all items, with 14 of 17 items ($r = .55$)

or greater, with a range from ($r = .49$) to ($r = .75$; Carlson, 2001). In the present study,

Cronbach's alpha for the SPTSS was .86 for the 68 participants that began the study.

Evidence of validity for the SPTSS has been mostly criterion-related. The SPTSS

is significantly associated with other measures of PTSD symptoms such as the Structured

Interview for Posttraumatic Stress Disorder ($r = .68$) and Symptom Checklist –

Posttraumatic Stress Disorder subscale ($r = .79$). ANOVA and post-hoc tests indicate that

higher STPSS scores are reported by those who report both a sexual and non-sexual

trauma compared to those who report either or no trauma. Finally, a mean cutoff score of

4.0 is associated with a diagnostic sensitivity of .94 and specificity of .60. Respondents

that meet the mean cutoff score of 4.0 will be eligible for participation in the present

investigation.

A brief *Demographic Questionnaire* (see Appendix D), given to each participant

at the first meeting, requested basic demographic information (gender, age, race, college

classification) as well as the number of visits to a health center, school clinic, or family

doctor within the past two months. The form also asked each participant to devise a code

name to be used for identification purposes in the study, to ensure anonymity. Next,

respondents described their most traumatic experience.

An *Essay Evaluation Form* (Francis & Pennebaker, 1992; see Appendix E)

consists of eight questions on a 7-point Likert scale (from 1 = "not at all", to 7 = "very

much") that ask how meaningful, emotional, and personal the writing was for the

participant, degree to which they talked with others, wanted to talk with others, and held back from talking to others about their traumatic experience, and how severe and influential the event was. Also, a yes or no question asked if the respondent expected a benefit from the writing. Finally, a box gave participants the chance to indicate if they were so upset by the writing that they need to be contacted immediately. This question was included as a means of safety; anyone who endorsed this question would have been given immediate evaluation and referral for treatment. This form has been utilized in previous studies of the writing paradigm (Deters & Range, 2003; Kovac & Range, 2000; Pennebaker, 1989).

The *Impact of Events Scale Revised* (IES-R; Weiss & Marmar, 1996) consists of 22 trauma symptoms (i.e., "I thought about it when I didn't mean to") that are scored depending on symptom frequency during the past week (from 0 = "not at all" to 4 = "extremely"). Higher scores indicate more symptoms. The IES-R is an amended version of the Impact of Events Scale (Horowitz, Wilner, & Alvarez, 1979), both of which are designed to yield a measure of subjective distress that an individual currently feels with regard to a certain stressful life event. The IES-R contains the original 15 IES items, with one item modified in the Avoidance subscale, one item added to the Intrusion subscale, and six new items added to comprise the hyperarousal subscale. The IES-R has three subscales: intrusion (8 items), avoidance (8 items), and hyperarousal (6 items). Thus, the IES-R gauges the amount of subjective distress in the three symptom clusters necessary for a diagnosis of PTSD. Also, the IES-R has been adapted for use in Spanish (Baguena, Belena, Armelia, Roldan, & Reig, 2001), French (Brunet, St. Hilaire, Jehel, & King, 2003), and Japanese (Asukai et al., 2002), which highlights the utilization of the IES-R in international research. The IES-R has been utilized in several writing studies (DeBrule &

Range, 2005; Deters & Range, 2003) and was utilized in the present study as a measure

of PTSD symptoms keyed to a specific traumatic event (see Appendix F).

The IES-R exhibits acceptable reliability. In a group of 439 emergency personnel

that were directly or indirectly involved in the Loma Prieta earthquake, correlation

coefficients across one year were .57 for the Intrusion subscale, .51 for the Avoidance

subscale, and .59 for the Hyperarousal subscale (Weiss & Marmar, 1996). Among 206

insurance workers who experienced the 1994 Northridge earthquake, test-retest

coefficients, over 6 months, were .94 for Intrusion, .89 for Avoidance, and .92 for

Hyperarousal (Weiss & Marmar, 1996). The subscales of the IES-R all possess good

internal consistency, with Cronbach's alpha ranging from .87 to .92 for Intrusion, .84 to

.86 for Avoidance, and .79 to .90 for Hyperarousal among Earthquake survivors (Weiss

& Marmar, 1996). Furthermore, the global IES-R exhibited excellent internal consistency

(Cronbach's alpha = .96) among community members and treatment-seeking combat

veterans, with internal consistency for subscales ranging from .87 to .94 (Creamer, Bell,

& Failla, 2003). In the present study, Cronbach's alpha for the IES-R was .92 for both

prewriting and follow-up.

Validity for the avoidance and intrusion subscales of the IES-R is derived from

validation of the IES. The IES has been reported to be a valid instrument for measuring

changes in subjective distress as a significant difference occurred between the mean IES

scores of individuals who had stress response syndromes ($M = 35.3$ for men and 42.1 for

women) and a group of medical students that conducted autopsies on cadavers ($M = 6.9$

for men and 12.7 for women; Horowitz et al., 1979). A two-way ANOVA indicated that stressed individuals scored higher than medical students for the global scores listed above, $F = 170.9, p < .0001$, as well as for the avoidance subscale, $F = 73.0, p < .0001$, and the intrusion subscale, $(F = 212.1, p < .0001$; Horowitz et al., 1979). Also, evidence of concurrent validity is significant correlations with the PCL-C ($r = .84, p < .001$; Creamer et al., 2003). Finally, the IES-R exhibited diagnostic sensitivity and positive predictive power of .90 or better and a diagnostic specificity and negative predictive power of .84 among 154 community members who varied in PTSD symptoms (Creamer et al., 2003). Thus, the IES-R exhibits acceptable reliability and validity for people who have experienced a trauma.

The *Posttraumatic Checklist – Civilian Version* (PCL-C; Weathers, Litz, Herman, Huska, & Keane, 1993) consists of 17 items assessing PTSD symptoms (i.e., "Feeling VERY UPSET when SOMETHING reminded you of the stressful experience from the past") that have occurred during the past 30 days. Items are scored on a 5-point Likert scale (from 1 = "Not at all" to 5 = "Extremely", and higher scores indicate more symptoms. The PCL-C was utilized in the present investigation as a measure of clinically significant PTSD symptoms that is not keyed to a specific trauma (See Appendix H; Weathers, et al., 1993).

Evidence of reliability includes strong internal consistency (Cronbach's alpha = .94) among 27 motor vehicle accident victims and 13 sexual assault victims (Blanchard, Jones-Alexander, Buckley, & Forneris, 1996). Also, test-retest coefficients range from .88 across one week among 31 college students to .68 across two weeks among 26 college students (Ruggiero, Del Ben, Scotti, & Rabalais, 2003). In the present study, Cronbach's alpha for the PCL-C was .89 for prewriting and follow-up.

Evidence of validity includes significant correlations with the Clinician Administered PTSD Scale (Blake et al., 1995) for the PCL-C total score ($r = .93$) among 27 motor vehicle accident victims and 13 sexual assault victims (Blanchard et al., 1996). Further evidence is significant correlations with the Mississippi Scale for PTSD, State-Trait Anxiety Inventory, and IES (Ruggiero et al., 2003). Evidence for the diagnostic capabilities of the PCL-C have been mixed, with some investigators suggesting a cutoff of 44 (Blanchard et al., 1996) and others suggesting a cutoff of 50 (Weathers et al., 1993). A recent review of the PCL-C affirmed that utilizing a cutoff score of 44 or 50 was associated with diagnostic efficiency above .90, provided that respondents endorse a minimum score of 3 or higher on each item (Ruggiero, et al., 2003). Also, investigations that have utilized a primary care sample have yielded strong diagnostic specificity for a cutoff of 50 yet a better diagnostic sensitivity for a cutoff of 28, suggesting that a cutoff ranging from 28 to 32 may be ideal for primary care settings (Lang, Laffaye, Satz, Dresselhaus, & Stein, 2003).

The *Posttraumatic Dissociation Scale* (PTD; Carlson & Waelde, 2000) consists of 24 items that gauge trauma-related dissociation (i.e., "I felt like I was in a movie – like nothing that was happening was real."). Items are scored on a 5-point Likert scale indicating the frequency of dissociative symptoms (from 0 = "not at all" to 10+ = "more than 10 times") during the past week. Higher scores indicate more dissociation. The PTD yields a total score as well as five subscales: Depersonalization, Derealization, Gaps in

Awareness, Amnesia, and Gaps in Awareness due to Reexperiencing. Unlike other widely used measures of dissociation, which measure general dissociation, the PTD is designed for use specifically with trauma victims. The PTD was utilized in the present investigation as a measure of trauma-related dissociation that is not keyed to a specific trauma (See Appendix G; Carlson & Waelde, 2000).

Evidence of reliability is strong internal consistency for the total score (Cronbach's alpha = .94) as well as acceptable internal consistency for each subscale (Cronbach's alpha = .84 - .76) among 62 veterans in a residential PTSD treatment program. Further evidence of reliability is strong internal consistency for the total score (Cronbach's alpha = .89) among 30 community members diagnosed with PTSD (Carlson & Waelde, 2000). In the present study, Cronbach's alpha for the PTD was .91 for prewriting and .86 for follow-up.

Evidence of validity is significant association with measures of PTSD and dissociation. The PTD total score was significantly correlated with the Clinician Administered PTSD scale $(r = .51)$ and the Dissociative Experiences Scale $(r = .56)$ in a combined sample of treatment seeking veterans and community members. The PTD was also significantly correlated with the Posttraumatic Checklist- Specific (Weathers et al., 1993) among 43 combat veterans $(r = .55, p > .0001)$. Furthermore, each subscale of the PTD was significantly correlated with each subscale of the Dissociative Experiences Scale $(r = .39$ to .57).

The *Linguistic Inquiry and Word Count* (LIWC; Pennebaker, Francis, & Booth, 2001) is a text analysis computer program that evaluates the content of writing samples.

The LIWC contains a database of 2,290 words in four main domains (emotional expression, cognitive strategies, content domains, and language composition) that are further divided into 40 categories. This program has been used consistently in literature that deals with the writing paradigm in order to make comparisons based on the content of the writing sample (Kovac & Range, 2000; Richards et al., 2000). This program provides the numerical value ratio for these 40 word categories based on a dictionary file of the program. The LIWC also calculates a percentage of these counts relative to the number of total words written, a feature that controls for differences in total words each individual writes. The LIWC measures positive emotion words such as *happy, pretty, and good*, negative emotion words such as *hate, worthless, and enemy*, and cognitive mechanism words, such as *cause, know and ought*. In the SLIWC dictionary, the positive emotion category consists of 261 words, the negative emotion category consists of 345 words, and the cognitive mechanism category consists of 312 words. In addition, 49 causal words, such as *because, effect*, and *hence*, as well as 116 insight words, such as *think, know*, and *consider*, provide a specific measure of cognitively oriented word usage. The present investigation will assess five word categories: positive emotion, negative emotion, insight, causal, and cognitive mechanism words (See Appendix I).

An *Experiment Evaluation Form* contained five questions on a 7-point Likert scale (from 1 = "none" to 7 = "a great deal") that asked about relevant behaviors that had occurred during the study, including three questions that asked participants how much they had thought about the study, talked to others about their participation, and valued the study and two questions that asked how much the writing process had improved their perspective or emotions relative to trauma. In addition to these five questions, an open-ended question asked how many doctor visits have occurred in the past six weeks. Finally, participants were given space to elaborate on specific changes, benefits, or harm they experienced due to writing during the study and to give suggestions for improving the study (see Appendix L).

Procedure

Participants were selected through use of the Screening Form, which included information about several aspects of trauma, including type, duration, frequency, and time since trauma occurred. Respondents who suffered a trauma 2 or more months ago that met DSM-IV criteria A for PTSD (American Psychiatric Association, 2002) were eligible to participate. Finally, respondents also had to have endorsed enough PTSD symptoms to obtain a cutoff score of 15 or higher on the SPTSS (Carlson & Waelde, 2001) to be eligible. Thus, respondents were considered for participation if they reported a trauma that occurred several months ago and current PTSD symptoms.

Pilot study

Prior to data collection, a pilot study was conducted to ensure that participants adequately understood informed consent, self-report measures, SUDS instructions, and writing instructions. The pilot study also was utilized to determine if participants experienced a noteworthy increase in SUDS during a 45-minute writing session about trauma. A SUDS scale of 50 or higher was utilized as the threshold indicative of a noteworthy degree of exposure in the pilot study.

Participants were asked to write for one session, and report SUDS at five minute intervals for forty five minutes of writing. Of the 10 participants selected for the pilot study, 8 participated, 1 failed to show on two occasions, and 1 declined participation after reading informed consent. Results indicated that writing about various traumas (combat, motor vehicle accident, witnessing critical injury) resulted in maximum SUDS scores equal to or above 50 for five of the eight participants. For the other three participants, two wrote about bereavement instead of trauma (max SUDS = 12 & 40) and one wrote about molestation (max SUDS = 40). Mean SUDS scores also exhibited a quadratic trend; SUDS were lowest at the beginning (M = 16.25), increased steadily up to minutes 20 (M = 42.00) and 25 (M = 44.38) and then decreased steadily until minute 45 (M = 32.4). One-way ANOVA (Minute: 0, 5, 10, 15, 20, 25, 30, 35, 40, & 45) was significant, F (8) = 13.37, p = .02, η^2 = .77, such that pilot writers reported more SUDS over time. ANOVA also indicated a significant quadratic effect, F (8) = 12.82, p = .02, η^2 = .76. However, some participants commented that the 45 minutes of writing was somewhat too long and three were excluded from analysis because they did not write for the entire 45 minutes as instructed. Therefore, instructions were modified such that participants in the present study engaged in exposure writing for 40 minutes in the primary study, exactly double the writing time of the writing paradigm and control conditions.

Primary study

The primary investigator contacted potential participants through email and/or phone calls and provided a brief description of the study. Those who choose to participate were randomly assigned to either the exposure, writing paradigm, or control condition.

Participants engaged in 4 days of participation: the primary investigator met with all participants on day 1 to explain the research in detail, and explain tasks involved in the study. For days 2, 3, and 4 participants met with either the primary investigator or a trained research assistant.

For Day 1, participants were given an informed consent form that outlined the procedure, benefits, and risks of participating in the present study. Next, participants completed a set of dependent measures in random order, including the IES-R, PDS, and PTD. Participants were then given a handout that provided an explanation of Subjective Units of Distress (SUDS; Wolpe, 1973) and lists a detailed hierarchy from 0-100 for participants to refer to throughout the study. The primary researcher then discussed the meaning and importance of SUDS in the present study, and gave examples of situations that could elicit a SUDS of 70 or 80. Next, participants were asked to identify an imagined situation that would elicit a SUDS score of over 50, and were given feedback as to the appropriateness of their response. The investigator allowed participants to read their writing instructions from a sealed envelope, and encouraged them to ask questions about their writing topic. The instructions remained with participants as they wrote in a quiet, private research area.

Participants were randomly assigned to one of three experimental conditions: exposure writing, the standard writing paradigm, or a control writing condition. Participants in the exposure writing condition received the following instructions:

> "Write about a time when you experienced or witnessed an event that involved death or the possibility of death or serious injury, where you felt intense fear or helplessness. Really get into it and freely express any and all emotions or thoughts that you have about the experience. Focus on the sensations that you felt during

the event (sights, sounds, smells). Please be sure to write about the same trauma each day of writing. If you get stuck, repeat yourself or go into greater detail. As you write, do not worry about punctuation or grammar, just really let go and write as much as you can about the experience."

Participants in the writing paradigm condition received the following instructions:

"Write about a time when you experienced or witnessed an event that involved death or the possibility of death or serious injury, where you felt intense fear or helplessness. Write about the experience in as much detail as you can. Really get into it and freely express any and all emotions or thoughts that you have about the experience. As you write, do not worry about punctuation or grammar, just really let go and write as much as you can about the experience."

Participants in the control condition received the following instructions:

"Write about your plans for the day. Write about your plans in as much detail as you can. If you get stuck, repeat yourself or go into greater detail. Focus on describing your topic as fully as possible. Try to be as objective as possible, sticking with facts and details. As you write, do not worry about punctuation or grammar, just write as much as you can about your plans. If you finish with your plans for the day, discuss your plans for tomorrow."

After completing questionnaires on Day 1, participants in the writing paradigm and control writing conditions wrote about their topic for 20 minutes, whereas participants in the exposure writing condition wrote for 40 minutes. Directly after writing, participants completed the Essay Evaluation Form.

During each writing session, subjective units of distress were reported before and throughout the writing time. As participants wrote, they listened to a recorded audiotape that provided a brief auditory cue for participants to report their SUDS level every five minutes. Thus, participants in the writing paradigm or control writing condition reported SUDS five times: prewriting and 5, 10, 15, and 20 minutes into the writing session.

Participants in the exposure writing condition reported SUDS nine times: prewriting and 5, 10, 15, 20, 25, 30, 35, and 40 minutes into the writing session.

At the completion of each day, participants scheduled a time to return for the subsequent day of participation, and were told that the investigator would call or send an email to remind them of their next appointment. The investigator also inspected the immediate care box on the Essay Evaluation Form prior to each participant's departure. The investigator also read all writing samples within 24 hours and ensured that no participant wrote about any suicidal ideation, imminent suicidal risk, or imminent homicidal risk. No participant requested an opportunity to speak with a mental health professional and no essay contained themes involving threat to self or others.

For Day 2, Day 3, and Day 4, participants wrote about their topic for 20 minutes (writing paradigm and control conditions) or 40 minutes (exposure condition), reported SUDS at five-minute intervals, and completed the Essay Evaluation Form. Participants were asked to schedule a consistent time for each week to write. No participant was allowed to write more than once in a week, and any participants who did not return to write within 14 days of participation were excluded. Thus, all participants completed a total of four writing sessions that occurred across approximately four weeks.

For follow-up, participants were contacted six weeks after completing writing, and completed measures approximately six to eight weeks after the final writing session. Participants completed the IES-R, PDS, and PTD, and Experiment Evaluation Form, and were paid $10.00 for participating in all phases of the research.

RESULTS

Prior to data analysis, written samples and dependent measures were scrutinized to ensure that participants followed directions. Of the 68 participants who began the study, 6 were excluded from the final analysis because they did not complete follow-up forms and 14 were excluded for not completing all four days of writing. This resulted in a final number of 48 participants. The attrition rate of the present study was approximately 30%. A one-way Analysis of Variance (ANOVA) indicated that group differences did not exist on any demographic variable or dependent measure prior to the writing intervention. ANOVA also indicated no significant pretest differences between participants who completed the study and participants who did not.

Manipulation Check

A manipulation check was conducted through analysis of the LIWC and the Essay Evaluation Form to ensure that each group followed writing instructions. LIWC word counts were evaluated through use of a 3 (Condition: Exposure, Writing Paradigm, and Control) X 4 (Essay: 1, 2, 3, 4) X 5 (Count: Negative Emotion, Positive Emotion, Cognitive Mechanism, Causal, and Insight) MANOVA. A significant interaction was found for condition X essay X count, $F(2, 45) = 1.95$, $p = .017$, $\eta^2 = .41$. MANOVA also indicated main effects for both essay, $F(2, 45) = 16.37$, $p < .001$, $\eta^2 = .53$, and word count, $F(2, 45) = 165.66$, $p < .001$, $\eta^2 = .94$. Finally, significant interactions were found between condition and word count, $F(2, 45) = 4.37$, $p < .001$, $\eta^2 = .29$, as well as essay and word count, $F(2, 45) = 69.57$, $p < .001$, $\eta^2 = .96$. Post-hoc analyses indicated that both the exposure and writing paradigm condition wrote more negative, positive, causal, cognitive mechanism, and insight words across essays than the control group ($p < .001$ for both contrasts).

Follow-up mixed-design repeated-measures ANOVA's for each word count were conducted following the significant interaction of condition, essay, and count. For positive words, ANOVA indicated a main effect for time (essay), $F(2, 45) = 3.85$, $p < .016$, $\eta^2 = .21$, but no main effect of condition or interaction. Follow-up analysis indicated that more positive words were used on Day 2 compared to Day 1 ($p = .018$), and on Day 2 compared to Day 4 ($p = .029$) For negative words, ANOVA indicated a significant main effect for time, $F(2, 45) = 41.15$, $p < .001$, $\eta^2 = .74$, a significant main effect for condition, $F(2, 45) = 3.39$, $p = .005$, $\eta^2 = .19$, and a significant interaction of time and condition, $F(2, 45) = 11.52$, $p < .001$, $\eta^2 = .34$. Follow-up analysis using Tukey's LSD indicated a significant difference between the exposure and control group ($p < .001$), and between the writing paradigm and control group ($p < .001$). Follow-up analysis also indicated that more negative words were used on Day 1 compared to Day 4, Day 2 compared to Day 4, and Day 3 compared to Day 4 (all $p < .001$). As predicted, the exposure and writing paradigm conditions did not differ in negative word usage across time, yet both conditions were found to yield more negative words than the control condition across time. In contrast, positive word usage was similar in all conditions, and more positive words were used in Day 2 compared to other days.

The remaining three LIWC counts all measured different aspects of cognitively oriented terms. For the most global measure, the cognitive mechanism count, ANOVA indicated a significant main effect for time, $F(2, 45) = 201.55$, $p < .001$, $\eta^2 = .93$, a significant main effect for condition, F (2, 45) = 70.8, $p < .001$, $\eta^2 = .36$, and a significant interaction of time and condition, F (2, 45) = 2.95, $p = .01$, $\eta^2 = .17$. Follow-up analyses indicated that more cognitive mechanism words were used by both the exposure condition ($p < .001$) and the writing paradigm condition ($p < .001$) when compared to the control condition. No difference was found between the exposure and writing paradigm conditions. Follow-up analysis also indicated that more cognitive mechanism words were used on Day 1 compared to Day 4, Day 2 compared to Day 4, and Day 3 compared to Day 4 (all $p < .001$).

The pattern found for overall cognitive words held for one specific cognitive count, causal words, but was somewhat different for another specific cognitive count, insight words. For the causal count, ANOVA indicated a significant main effect for time, F (2, 45) = 134.37, $p < .001$, $\eta^2 = .90$, a significant main effect for condition, F (2, 45) = 17.8, $p < .001$, $\eta^2 = .33$, and a significant interaction of time and condition, F (2, 45) = 4.04, $p = .001$, $\eta^2 = .22$. Follow-up analyses indicated significant differences between the exposure condition and control condition (p = .002) as well as between the writing paradigm condition and the control condition (p < .001), but not between the exposure and writing paradigm conditions.

For the insight count, ANOVA indicated a significant main effect for time, F (2, 45) = 9.21, $p < .001$, $\eta^2 = .39$, a significant main effect for condition, F (2, 45) = 21.4, $p < .001$, $\eta^2 = .43$, but no significant interaction of time and condition. Follow-up analyses indicated that more insight words were used by both the exposure condition (p < .001) and the writing paradigm condition (p < .001) when compared to the control condition. No difference was found between the exposure and writing paradigm conditions. Follow-up analysis also indicated that more insight words were used on Day 1 compared to Day 4, Day 2 compared to Day 4, and Day 3 compared to Day 4 (all $p <$ .001; See Table 1).

Table 1.

ANOVAs for Five Primary LIWC Counts.

Source	df	F	p	η^2	Post-hoc
Positive Emotion					
Condition (C)	2	NS			
Time (T)	2	3.85	.16	.21	2 > 1, 2 > 4
C X T	45	NS			
Negative Emotion					
Condition (C)	2	3.39	.005	.19	E > C, WP > C
Time (T)	2	41.15	<.001	.74	1 > 4, 2 > 4, 3 > 4
C X T	45	11.52	<.001	.34	
Cognitive Mechanism					
Condition (C)	2	70.8	<.001	.36	E > C, WP > C
Time (T)	2	201.55	<.001	.93	1 > 4, 2 > 4, 3 > 4
C X T	45	2.95	.01	.17	
Causal					
Condition (C)	2	17.8	<.001	.33	E > C, WP > C
Time (T)	2	134.37	<.001	.90	3 > 1, 4 > 1, 4 > 2, 4 > 3
C X T	45	4.04	.001	.22	
Insight					
Condition (C)	2	21.4	<.001	.43	E > C, WP > C
Time (T)	2	9.21	<.001	.39	1 > 4, 2 > 4, 3 > 4
C X T	45	NS			

Note: Exposure Condition =E, Writing Paradigm Condition = WP, Control Condition = C, Day = 1-4

For the Essay Evaluation Form, a 3 (Condition: Exposure, Writing Paradigm, Control) X 4 (Time: Day 1, Day 2, Day 3, Day 4) Mixed-Design Repeated Measures ANOVA was completed for each of 8 questions. For the question regarding how personal the essay was, ANOVA indicated no significant effect for time, condition, or interaction, although the main effect for condition approached significance, $F(2, 45) = 2.72$, $p = .08$, $\eta^2 = .11$. For the question regarding how meaningful the essay was, ANOVA indicated a significant effect for time, $F(2, 45) = 3.51, p = .027, \eta^2 = .07$, such that all conditions reported increased meaning over time. ANOVA also indicated a main effect for condition, $F(2, 45) = 6.27, p = .004, \eta^2 = .22$, but no significant interaction for time and condition. Tukey's LSD post-hoc tests indicated a significant difference between the exposure condition ($M = 5.82$) and the control condition ($M = 4.08$; p = .003), and the writing paradigm condition ($M = 5.72$) and the control condition ($p = .004$), but no significant difference between the exposure and writing paradigm conditions. For the question regarding the severity of the topic, ANOVA indicated a significant effect for condition, $F(2, 45) = 25.76, p < .001, \eta^2 = .54$, but no significant effect for time or interaction. Tukey's LSD post-hoc tests indicated a significant difference between the exposure condition ($M = 5.85$) and the control condition ($M = 2.89$; p < .001), and the writing paradigm condition ($M = 5.82$) and the control condition (p < .001), but no significant difference between the exposure and writing paradigm conditions. For the question regarding how much emotion was revealed in the essay, ANOVA indicated a significant effect for condition, $F(2, 45) = 4.89, p = .01, \eta^2 = .18$, but no significant effect for time or interaction. Tukey's LSD post-hoc tests indicated a significant difference between the Exposure condition ($M = 5.4$) and the Control Condition ($M = 3.75$; p = .005), and the Writing Paradigm condition ($M = 5.06$) and the Control Condition (p = .02), but no significant difference between the exposure and writing paradigm conditions. For the question regarding actively holding back from talking about the topic, ANOVA indicated a significant effect for condition, $F(2, 45) = 6.08, p = .005, \eta^2 = .21$, but no significant effect for time or interaction. Tukey's LSD post-hoc tests indicated a significant difference between the Exposure condition ($M = 4.28$) and the Control Condition ($M = 2.48$; $p = .002$), and the Exposure Condition and Writing Paradigm condition ($M = 2.96$; $p = .015$), but no significant difference between the writing paradigm and control conditions. For the questions regarding if the topic is still affecting the writer's life, talking with others about the topic, and wanting to talk with others about the topic, ANOVA indicated no significant effect for time, condition, or interaction.

Exploratory post-hoc analysis of LIWC counts involving sensory details was also completed, unrelated to the manipulation check. This was completed in order to determine if prompting the exposure condition to focus on sensory details of the trauma led to differences compared to the writing paradigm condition.

Four specific word counts were analyzed by 2 (Condition: Exposure & Writing paradigm) X 4 (Time: Day 1, 2, 3, & 4) repeated-measures ANOVAs for overall sensory words, then for three specific sensory counts. For overall sensory words, ANOVA indicated a significant main effect of time, $F(1, 31) = 15.63$, $p < .001$, $\eta^2 = .63$, but no significant main effect of condition or interaction of time and condition. Follow-up analysis indicated that both conditions tended to write less sensory words over time, and that the most significant decrease occurred from Day 3 ($M = 3.05$ for exposure, $M = 2.51$ for writing paradigm) to Day 4 ($M = 1.61$ for exposure, $M = 1.19$ for writing paradigm).

For hearing words, this pattern held, as ANOVA indicated a main effect for time, $F(1, 31) = 11.36$, $p < .001$, $\eta^2 = .55$, but no main effect for condition or any interaction. Follow-up analyses also revealed a similar trend, in that both conditions used about the same number of hearing words on Days 1, 2, and 3, but then used significantly fewer

hearing words on Day 4. For seeing words, ANOVA indicated a significant main effect

for time, $F(1, 31) = 42.52$, $p < .001$, $\eta^2 = .82$, but no significant main effect for condition

or interaction of time and condition. In contrast to analysis for sensory and hearing

words, follow-up analysis indicated that both conditions used more hearing words over

time, specifically from Day 3 (Exposure $M = .84$, Writing Paradigm $M = .58$) to Day 4

(Exposure $M = 2.58$, Writing Paradigm $M = 2.61$).

For feeling words, ANOVA indicated a significant main effect for time, $F(1, 31)$

$= 42.52$, $p < .001$, $\eta^2 = .82$, but no significant main effect for condition, $F(1, 31) = 2.62$,

$p = .055$, $\eta^2 = .08$, or interaction of time and condition. Follow-up analysis indicated no

significant difference for Days 1, 2, and 3, but a significant increase in feeling words on

Day 4.

The present study requested that participants in one condition focus on sensory

details of the trauma during writing. However, those in the exposure condition did not use

significantly more sensory details than the condition that received the standard writing

paradigm instructions. Linguistic analysis indicated that present exposure instructions did

not result in increased usage of sense-related words (e.g. sights or sounds) compared to

standard writing paradigm instructions.

Dependent Measures

The primary hypothesis of the present study was that those who write about a

trauma will exhibit a significant decrease in PTSD symptoms and trauma-related

dissociation compared to those who write about a control topic. In order to evaluate this hypothesis, all primary measures of interest were evaluated by conducting a 3 (Condition: Exposure, Writing Paradigm, Control) X 2 (Time: Prewriting and Follow-Up) X 3 (Measure: IES-R, PDS, and PTD) mixed-design repeated measures MANOVA, which did not indicate an interaction of condition, time, and measure, $F(2, 1, 45) = 1.53$, $p = .20$, $\eta^2 = .07$. MANOVA did indicate a significant interaction for time and measure, $F(2, 45) = 6.96$, $p = .002$, $\eta^2 = .91$, but not for time and condition or measure and condition. MANOVA also indicated a main effect for measure, $F(2, 45) = 308.28$, $p < .001$, $\eta^2 = .93$, and for time, $F(2, 45) = 48.01$, $p < .001$, $\eta^2 = .52$, but no main effect for condition. Follow-up analysis indicated that all conditions reported fewer symptoms from prewriting to follow-up for all three measures. Therefore, the general pattern of the main MANOVA indicated no significant differences between conditions, which fails to confirm the main hypothesis of the study. All participants exhibited a trend towards experiencing fewer symptoms of PTSD and dissociation as time progressed, regardless of condition (See Table 2 for means).

Further analyses were conducted on each individual measure to determine specific condition differences that may not have been evident in the MANOVA. For each dependent measure, a mixed-design repeated measures 3 (Condition: Exposure, Writing Paradigm, and Control) X 2 (Time: Prewriting and Follow-Up) Analysis of Variance (ANOVA) was completed. Each of the three ANOVA's indicated a main effect for time for the IES-R, $F(2, 45) = 37.87$, $p < .001$, $\eta^2 = .46$, PTD, $F(2, 45) = 20.84$, $p < .001$, $\eta^2 = .32$, and PCL-C, $F(2, 45) = 43.81$, $p < .001$, $\eta^2 = .49$. However, no significant effect for condition or interaction of condition and time was found for any of the dependent measures. Also, follow-up analyses for each individual dependent measure indicated that participants experienced a decrease in negative symptoms over time regardless of condition.

Table 2.

Means and (Standard Deviations) for Dependent Measures at Prewriting and Follow-up

Condition	Exposure		Writing Paradigm		Control	
	Pre	Follow-up	Pre	Follow-up	Pre	Follow-up
IES-R Total	36.93	25.93	33.58	15.17	42.12	25.56
	(21.48)	(14.59)	(18.09)	(10.18)	(15.72)	(16.15)
Intrusion	14.40	10.07	12.18	4.94	15.94	8.12
	(8.30)	(4.96)	(7.94)	(3.19)	(6.73)	(5.29)
Avoidance	13.60	11.33	14.17	5.88	15.69	10.93
	(8.78)	(5.94)	(7.55)	(4.88)	(6.24)	(6.69)
Hyperarousal	8.93	4.53	7.29	4.35	10.50	6.25
	(6.67)	(4.86)	(5.44)	(3.52)	(5.02)	(5.21)
PTD	20.67	11.07	18.53	8.94	21.06	14.19
	(12.67)	(10.64)	(13.38)	(7.37)	(13.94)	(9.61)
PCL-C	44.07	33.40	40.65	27.85	48.06	31.50
	(18.72)	(12.72)	(10.50)	(4.80)	(14.14)	(10.50)
Health Visits	1.07	1.13	0.59	0.82	2.63	1.50
	(2.6)	(1.36)	(.71)	(.88)	(5.34)	(1.75)

Another hypothesis was that those who write about a trauma will report fewer health visits than those who write about a control topic. A 3 (Condition: Exposure, Writing Paradigm, and Control) X 2 (Time: Prewriting, Follow-up) mixed-design repeated-measures ANOVA was conducted to test for differences in health visits between conditions. Contrary to hypothesis, ANOVA failed to detect a significant interaction of time and condition, $F(2, 45) = .70$, $p = .52$, or a main effect of time, $F(2, 45) = .29$,

$p = .60$, or condition, $F(2, 45) = 2.17$, $p = .13$. However, Levene's test of Equality was

significant for pretest health visits, indicating unequal variance among conditions. Pretest

health visits were much higher for the control condition ($M = 2.63$) compared to the

experimental conditions ($M = 1.07$ and $.59$; See Table 3). When one outlier was removed

from the analysis, ANOVA found a main effect for time that was not significant,

$F(2, 45) = 3.27$, $p = .08$, $\eta^2 = .07$. Health visits did not respond to the writing

intervention for any condition.

SUDS Ratings and Experiment Evaluation

The present study was the first writing paradigm study to explore continuous

SUDS ratings during writing. Therefore, exploratory analyses for SUDS ratings of each

day were conducted by a 3 (Condition: Exposure, Writing Paradigm, and Control) X 4

(Time: Day 1, 2, 3, or 4) X 5 (SUDS score: prewriting, 5, 10, 15, 20 minutes during

writing) mixed-design repeated-measures MANOVA. A significant interaction was

expected in which exposure and writing paradigm writers report lower SUDS across time

compared to control writers. MANOVA failed to indicate a significant interaction of

condition, time and SUDS, $F(2, 3, 45) = .94$, $p = .56$, $\eta^2 = .25$. MANOVA did indicate a

significant interaction for condition and time, $F(2, 45) = 2.84$, $p = .014$, $\eta^2 = .17$, such

that exposure and writing paradigm conditions reported decreasing SUDS ratings across

the multiple essays, whereas the control condition reported no change. MANOVA also

indicated a significant interaction for condition and SUDS, $F(2, 45) = 4.66$, $p < .001$,

$\eta^2 = .31$, but not for time and SUDS. Follow-up analysis indicated that SUDS gradually increased as time went by during a writing session for the exposure and writing paradigm

conditions, but did not change significantly for the control condition writing. Finally,

MANOVA indicated a main effect for time, $F(2, 45) = 6.42, p < .001, \eta^2 = .31$, and for

SUDS, $F(2, 45) = 11.99, p < .001, \eta^2 = .53$, but not for condition. Condition means of

Mean SUDS for All Conditions

Day 1

From minute 0-20

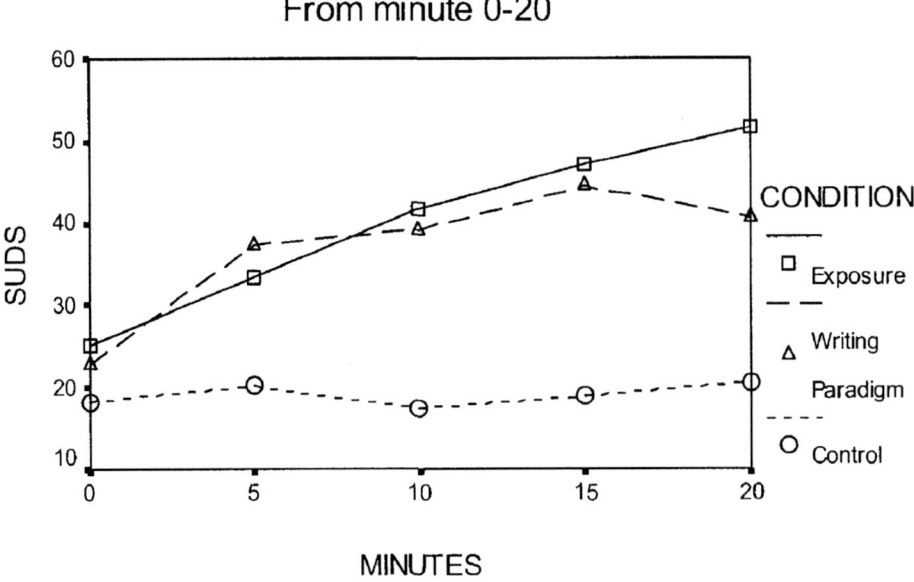

Figure 1. *Mean SUDS for Exposure, Writing Paradigm, and Control Conditions on Day 1*

SUDS scores indicated that ratings generally decreased across each writing session for all

conditions, and that both experimental conditions experienced lower SUDS over time

compared to the control condition (See Figures 1-4). Also, both experimental conditions reported an increase in SUDS every five minutes from prewriting to 20 minutes, whereas

the control condition reported no within session change in SUDS.

For the exposure condition, the additional 4 SUDS ratings (9 total) for each day

were analyzed with a 4 (Day: 1, 2, 3, or 4) X 9 (Minutes: prewriting, 5, 10, 15, 20, 25, 30,

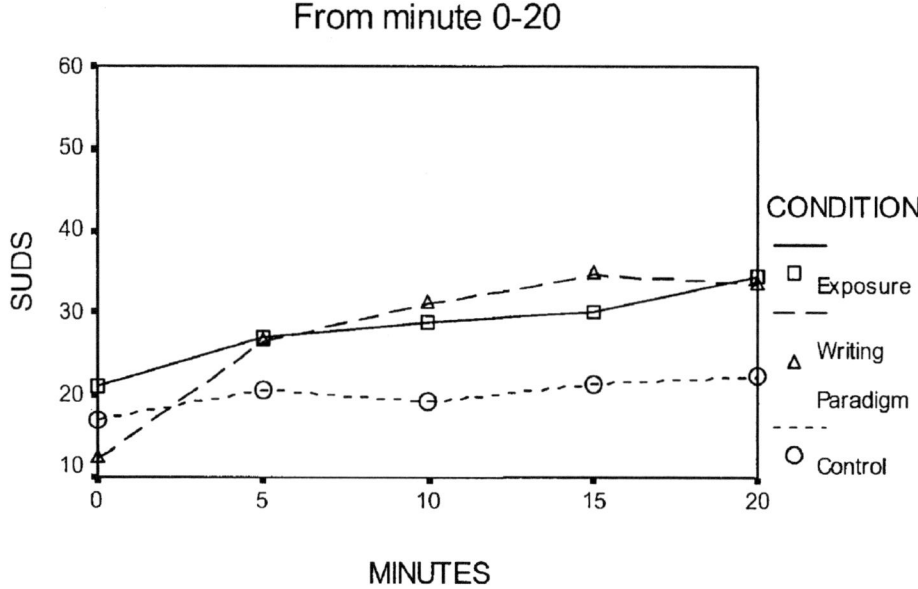

Mean SUDS for All Conditions

Day 2

From minute 0-20

Figure 2. *Mean SUDS for Exposure, Writing Paradigm, and Control Conditions on Day 2.*

35, and 40 minutes during writing) repeated-measures ANOVA. Prior to analysis, three

participants were excluded from analysis because they failed to report at least one SUDS

rating during minutes 25- 40. ANOVA indicated a significant main effect for Day,

$F(3, 8) = 7.23, p = .009, \eta^2 = .71$, and a significant main effect for Minutes, $F(3, 8) = 11.84, p < .001, \eta^2 = .52$, but no significant interaction. Participants in the exposure condition reported less average SUDS across each day of writing, yet increasing SUDS from the beginning to end of each writing session. A quadratic effect for minutes was

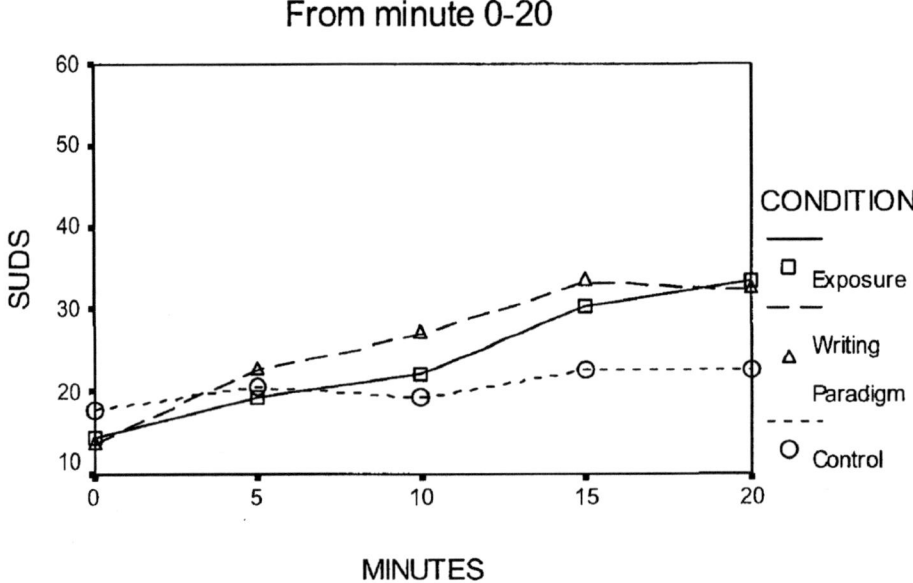

Figure 3. *Mean SUDS for Exposure, Writing Paradigm, and Control Conditions on Day 3.*
found, $F(3, 8) = 29.45, p < .001, \eta^2 = .73$, such that exposure writers tended to report more SUDS in the middle of the writing session and less SUDS at the beginning and end of writing during each session (See Figures 5-8).

Thus, when comparing this additional SUDS analysis for minutes 25-40 with the

main MANOVA, a specific trend for each condition emerged within the writing session.

The exposure condition exhibited an increase then decrease in SUDS, whereas the

writing paradigm condition only exhibited increasing SUDS, and the control condition

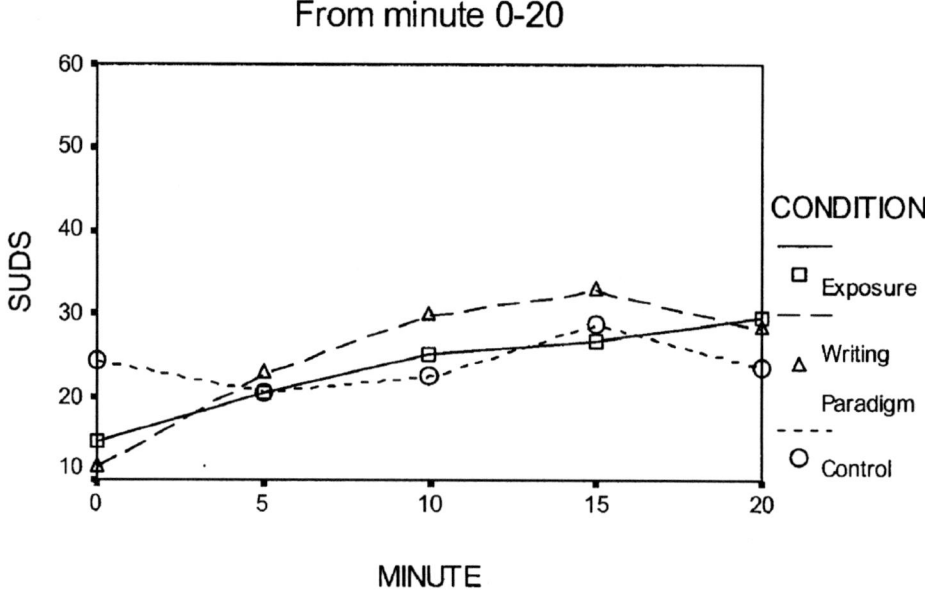

Mean SUDS for All Conditions

Day 4

From minute 0-20

Figure 4. *Mean SUDS for Exposure, Writing Paradigm, and Control Conditions on Day 4.*

exhibited no change. This overall pattern was consistent with hypothesis, such that

exposure writing resulted an expected peak and resolution of SUDS ratings within

session, whereas the writing paradigm resulted only in increasing SUDS ratings.

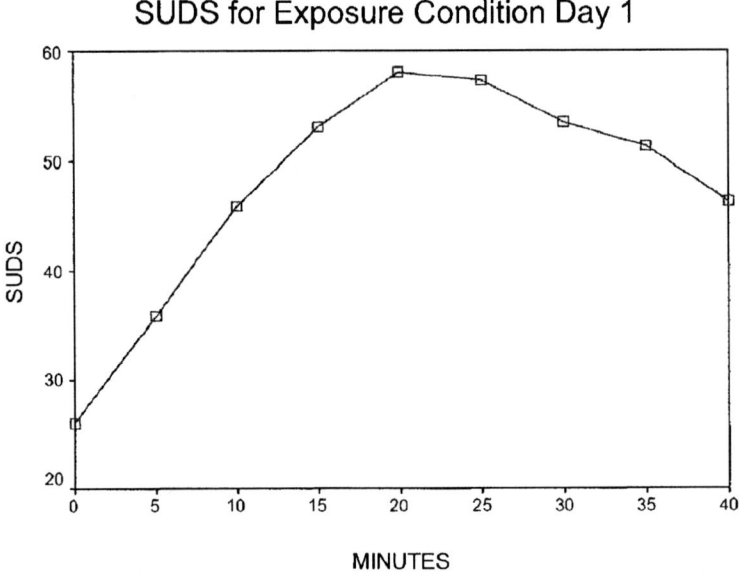

Figure 5. *SUDS for Exposure Condition on Day 1, From Minute 0-40.*

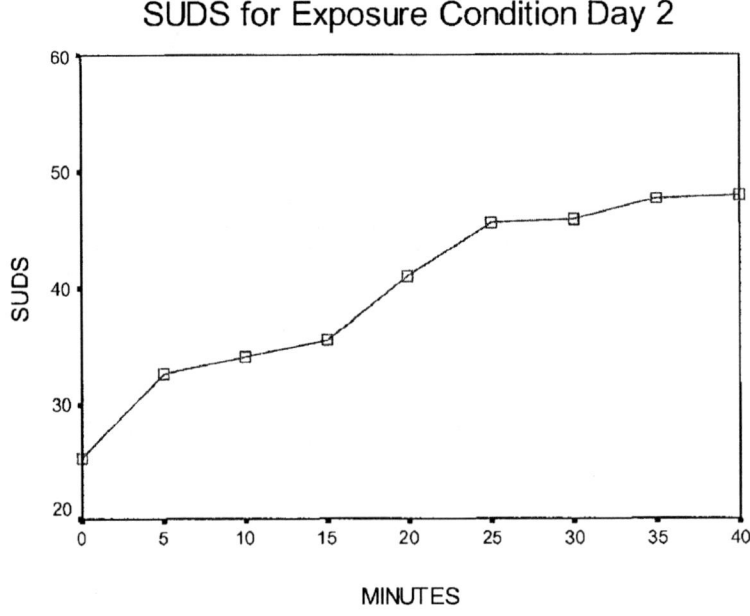

Figure 6. *SUDS for Exposure Condition on Day 2, From Minute 0-40.*

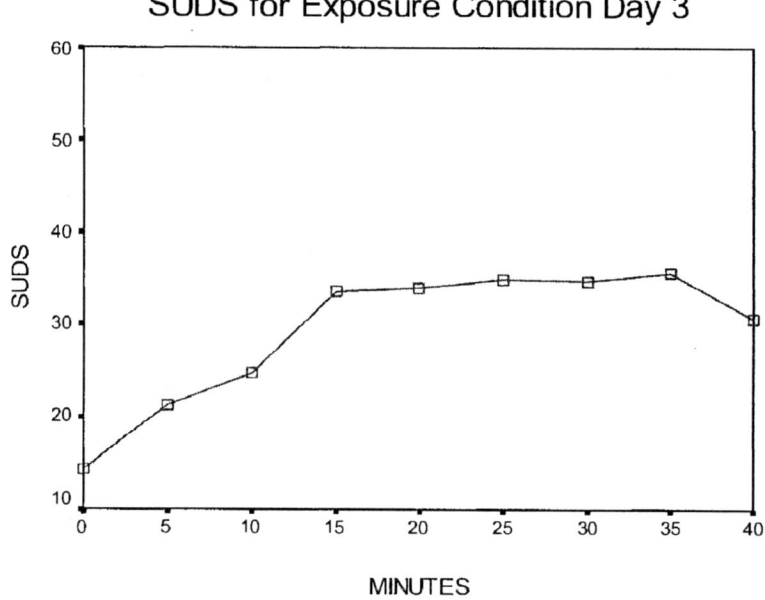

Figure 7. *SUDS for Exposure Condition on Day 3, From Minute 0-40.*

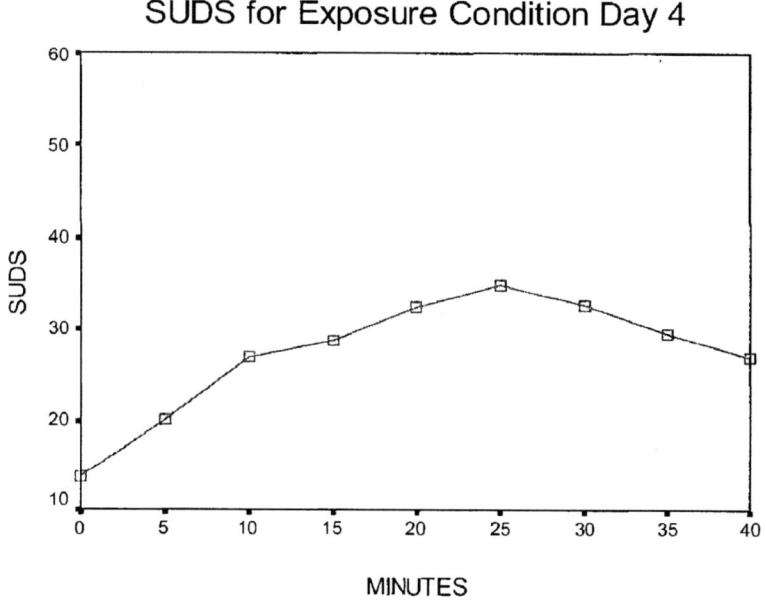

Figure 8. *SUDS for Exposure Condition on Day 4, From Minute 0-40.*

The Experiment Evaluation Form was analyzed to detect group differences in subjective ratings of the effects of the present study. A one-way ANOVA was completed for each of 5 Likert scale questions on the Experiment Evaluation Form (Bonferroni corrected to the .01 level). The exposure and writing paradigm conditions were expected to report that they thought and talked about the study more than the control group, and that they found the study to be more valuable compared to the control condition. The exposure and writing paradigm conditions were also expected to claim that writing has influenced their perspective and emotions relative to trauma compared to the control group. However, ANOVA failed to detect any significant differences between conditions for each of the five Experiment Evaluation Form questions: thought about the study, F (2, 45) = 2.36, p = .11, talked about the study, F (2, 45) = .59, p = .56, value of the study, F (2, 45) = .81, p = .45, perspective of trauma, F (2, 45) = 1.23, p = .30, and emotions related to trauma, F (2, 45) = 1.88, p = .16. Thus, participants reported similar ratings for the value, social impact, emotional impact, cognitive impact, and thought associated with the present study regardless of writing topic.

DISCUSSION

The main hypothesis of the present study was that exposure writing will lead to a decrease in symptoms of PTSD and dissociation, and that this decrease would be greater than that seen in the standard writing paradigm and control writing groups. The main hypothesis was not supported. Although the exposure writing group did show a decrease in symptoms of PTSD and dissociation, so did all participants who completed the study, regardless of writing topic (condition). Also, health visits decreased over time for all participants regardless of condition. Although these three findings were contrary to hypothesis, they are similar to the two other previous investigations conducted at the present university that examined a writing intervention in a trauma sample (DeBrule & Range, 2005; Deters & Range, 2003).

The present study involved several significant design components typical of writing paradigm studies: a manipulation check was conducted through linguistic analysis and essay ratings, two main dependent measures were assessed (PTSD and dissociation), and health visits were assessed. The present study was unique in comparison to the writing paradigm literature in three main regards: methodological changes were made to create an additional writing condition, many present screened participants may have suffered from the direct and indirect effects of Hurricane Katrina, and present findings are in contrast to other writing studies that have reported efficacy for writing in the context of trauma and PTSD. Finally, there were some promising findings of the present study that call for specific design changes that should be evaluated in future writing studies that aim to utilize exposure for PTSD symptoms and other trauma-related outcomes, such as dissociation, depression, and generalized anxiety.

Manipulation Check

A manipulation check was performed in the present study by use of linguistic analysis (LIWC), essay ratings, and SUDS scores. Most of these analyses confirmed the manipulation check, yet some specific measures failed to confirm the manipulation check. These discrepancies may indicate methodological flaws in the present study, and the resulting lack of condition differences for dependent measures. Most analyses indicated that those in the exposure or writing paradigm condition reported higher word counts, higher essay ratings on the Essay Evaluation Form, and higher SUDS scores compared to those in the control condition. Thus, participants generally followed writing instructions by writing about a trauma for either 40 or 20 minutes or writing about their plans for the day. Also, the primary investigator read all essays in the study, and determined that all essays matched the writing topic and were at least 100 words long. However, some analyses that typically indicate differences between trauma and control conditions failed to do so in the present study, suggesting that the control topic may have unexpectedly resulted in some emotional or cognitive processing.

The majority of linguistic counts indicated that more emotional or cognitive words were used in the exposure and writing paradigm conditions compared to the control condition. Consistent with expectations, participants that wrote about trauma tended to use more words involving negative emotion, cognitive mechanisms, insight, and causal relationships over time than participants that wrote about a control topic. Thus, participants in the exposure and writing paradigm conditions did appear to write about trauma. Unexpectedly, there was no difference in positive word usage for any of the three conditions, yet this LIWC count may not provide the best indication of adherence to present instructions. This finding may have also been due to participants in the control conditions focusing little on positive emotions associated with their plans for the day. Overall, four of five linguistic analyses indicated that the manipulation check held.

Responses for the Essay Evaluation form yielded mixed results. Consistent with expectations, participants in the exposure and writing paradigm conditions reported that their essays were more meaningful, more emotional, involved a more severe topic, and that they held back from talking about the essays more than participants in the control condition. However, unexpectedly, there were no differences between conditions for ratings of how personal the essay was, if the event described is still affecting their life, and if they wanted to or had talked to others about the topic. This suggests that the control topic allowed for personal information that is presently affecting the individual to be divulged, although this was not intended. Analysis of the Essay Evaluation Form mostly supported the manipulation check, but also suggests a lack of integrity for the specific control topic utilized in the present study. This finding suggests that some control instructions may have accidentally led to profound writing. This specific manipulation error may also help explain why participants in the control condition experienced similar improvement to participants in the exposure condition and the writing paradigm condition.

SUDS scores were not intended to provide a manipulation check, but overall

SUDS scores were significantly lower in for those in the control condition compared to the two conditions that wrote about trauma. This indicates that participants in all conditions were adhering to their topic. Also, SUDS scores did not change appreciably during the writing session for those in the control topic, yet tended to increase for the first 20 minutes in the trauma writing conditions. This suggests that although the control topic may have led to unintended emotional processing, the control condition did not report significant changes in anxiety during writing. This pattern was anticipated, but yet the improvement on dependent measures noted for the control condition was unanticipated. Although present changes in anxiety during exposure writing are consistent with exposure models, present findings suggest that improvement may occur for writing participants regardless of changes in anxiety.

The use of LIWC counts, the Essay Evaluation Form, and SUDS scores indicated that, for the most part, the experimental manipulations seemed to function appropriately. However, several discrepancies were noted, particularly on essay ratings, which may indicate that the control topic was too open ended and may have allowed participants to discuss personal thoughts and feelings related to their plans for the day. In other words, at least for some participants, the control writing might have actually functioned as more of a profound writing condition. This was evident in several control essays. For example, one participant wrote about checking the weather and described how her hometown was no longer on the weather map following Katrina. Another participant wrote that his main plan for the day was to obtain his FEMA check in order to meet financial obligations, and detailed the frustration and concern he was experiencing. Some of the profound content that was unintentionally detailed in the "plans for the day" of the control condition may have been unavoidable due to the post-disaster environment in which the study participants lived. In other words, control writers may naturally write about traumatic content if they are currently experiencing the aftermath of a widespread trauma, such as a natural disaster. For future writing investigations, the use of a more mundane control topic, such as the physical details of certain objects, and instructing control participants to avoid thoughts and feelings, may be more advantageous.

Effect of Writing on PTSD Symptoms and Dissociation

Present findings failed to find exclusive benefits for an exposure-based writing intervention, but did find that all writers experienced a decrease in PTSD symptoms regardless of writing topic. The lack of effect in the present study may have been affected by three specific design flaws. One, the control topic may have allowed for emotional and cognitive processing that typically occurs in treatment conditions. Two, the instructions and writing time for the exposure condition may not have resulted in adequate exposure. Three, the power of the study was lower than anticipated due to a high rate of attrition following unexpected circumstances, yet the small present effect size for primary analyses suggests that an increase in power may not have led to significance.

One unexpected trend that could explain present results was that the control condition seemed to engage in some emotional expression, as indicated by some essay and experiment ratings. This may have occurred because present writers often wrote about stressful or pleasurable aspects of their plans, and some wrote about aspects of Hurricane Katrina. Emotional expression is often cited as the most salient aspect of the writing paradigm, which is also referred to as "written emotional disclosure" (Sloan et al., 2005, p. 549). Also, control writers were aware that they may have to write about their most severe trauma before participating and completed several trauma related measures, which could have resulted in some unintentional cognitive processing of the trauma. Finally, control writers may have responded to placebo effects since they were told that writing about their plans for the day is a useful exercise. Therefore, one possible reason that participants in all three conditions reported improvement for PTSD and dissociation is that they may have all engaged in some degree of emotional expression and cognitive processing of a trauma or stressful topic, which may have led to anticipated benefits through habituation.

A second possible reason that all conditions improved equally concerns the strength of the exposure that writers experienced in the exposure condition. Although SUDS analyses indicated that exposure writing led to decreases in anxiety, other analysis indicated no significant difference in PTSD symptoms, dissociation, or any linguistic count for exposure writing compared to the writing paradigm. Furthermore, the writing paradigm condition reported somewhat lower means for PTSD symptoms compared to the exposure condition, although this difference was not statistically significant (See Table 2). Thus, the exposure condition did not appear to experience additional emotional expression or related additional benefits when compared to other conditions, which may partially explain the lack effect for condition.

A third reason for the lack of effect is the limited power of the present study. Pretest power analysis indicated that the present study required approximately 75 participants for power to equal .80. Although 796 students were screened, many opted

not to participate or failed to meet criteria. A total of 68 began participation; only 48

participants completed all phases of the present study, resulting in compromised power.

However, analysis of primary dependent measures indicated a remarkably small effect

size, $\eta^2 = .07$, which suggests that condition differences were very unlikely to have

existed if power was higher. The primary reason that the present study utilized a small

sample was that the primary MANOVA analysis was not statistically significant, and did

not exhibit a trend towards significance ($p = .20$). Present findings most likely would

have held if the final sample and power was increased, therefore no further data was

collected. Thus, it is most likely that the present study suffered more from the unexpected

design problems and responses of present participants, rather than lack of power.

Although three specific methodological issues may have limited treatment

integrity, the lack of effect in the present study may also indicate poor efficacy of the

present design. Writing about trauma may not be effective because the modality does not

confer the quality of exposure that is inherent in empirically supported treatments that

involve spoken exposure (Foa et al., 1991). Thus, in addition to several design flaws, a

second competing explanation for the general ineffectiveness of the intervention is that

the writing paradigm and permutations of the writing paradigm may not be a sufficient

treatment for traumatic stress.

Numerous other studies have been consistent with present findings, indicating that

all participants reported improvement over time on PTSD measures (Deters & Range,

2003; DeBrule & Range, 2005; Smyth et al., 2008) or that neither experimental or control writers reported improvement (Brown & Hiemberg, 2001; Batten et al., 2002). However, there are a few tightly controlled studies that have found improvement exclusively for the writing paradigm condition compared to a control condition (Sloan et al., 2005; Sloan & Marx, 2004), suggesting that writing studies must exhibit strong treatment integrity to have an effect. These studies have screened for trauma and utilized the writing paradigm, similar to the present study. However, in contrast to the present study, these investigations have involved three consecutive daily writing sessions, assessed cortisol, and measured PTSD symptoms with the Posttraumatic Diagnostic Scale (Sloan et al., 2005; Sloan & Marx, 2004). Investigations that have screened for trauma, reported low attrition rates, and assessed numerous dependent measures have been the most likely to find an effect for the trauma writing but not for control writing on measures such as PTSD symptoms, depression, cortisol, and general health (Sloan et al., 2005; Sloan & Marx, 2004; Smyth, et al., 2008).

Health Visits

General health was assessed in the present study as self-reported health visits, which have been examined consistently in writing paradigm investigations. A recent meta-analysis of 30 writing paradigm studies found that the intervention (Writing Paradigm vs. Control) leads to reduced health care utilization in healthy samples, but not those exposed to illness or psychological stressors (Harris, 2006). In the present study, health visits did not differ between conditions, but did exhibit a general trend of improving over time for all conditions. This finding is in contrast to many investigations that have found beneficial effects for the writing paradigm on health visits (Harris, 2006;

Richards et al., 2000) and more specific health measures, such as lung function in asthmatics (Smyth et al., 2000). However, many studies at the present university have failed to detect group differences in health visits following the writing paradigm (Antal & Range, 2005; DeBrule & Range, 2005; Deters & Range, 2002; Kovac & Range, 2000; Range et al., 2000). The lack of effect noted for present participants could have been due to three factors: disinhibition occurring in all conditions, the use of an inadequate health measure, and unexpected statistical anomalies.

Many of the predominant theories regarding the writing paradigm suggest that the reason participants experience health-related benefits is because of disinhibition. The disinhibition theory (Francis & Pennebaker, 1992) states that writing about trauma is helpful because it allows the writer to release the burdensome information related to the trauma, which would ordinarily result in compromised immune function. Control writers may have experienced additional benefits from writing about more general stressors and detailing pleasurable activities they plan to engage in. Given that participants as a whole tended to report less health visits from prewriting to follow-up, health visits may have decreased due to this factor. Participants in the control condition also experienced a decrease in PTSD symptoms and dissociation, which may have adversely affected health prewriting. Some participants in the control condition reported that the experiment was valuable, and many detailed information regarding current stressors, difficulties, or concerns in their essays about their plans for the day. Therefore, the finding that health visits responded to writing about trauma or their plans for the day may be the result of disinhibition of distressing information that is either trauma-related or ongoing. The use of a more mundane, non-emotional topic for the control condition could result in more significant group differences in health outcomes.

Writing about various topics did not result in differential health benefits in the present study, yet many studies have found effects on very specific dependent measures. In the current study, health was only assessed with one question, and responses may have varied based on the respondents' notion of a "health visit". The primary focus of the present study was to assess change in variables related to PTSD, and instructions were altered specifically for change in trauma-related variables. Therefore, specific measures that relate to trauma as well as health may be more likely to indicate change. For example, blood pressure and heart rate could have been assessed both as dependent measures as well as process variables. Finally, to better assess general health, future writing investigations should consider more comprehensive health measures such as the Pennebaker Inventory of Limbic Languidness (e.g., Richards et al., 2002).

The present lack of effect for health visits may have also been impacted by two unexpected statistical anomalies. One, unequal variance existed between conditions at prewriting, which may have affected ANOVA. Two, condition means were much higher for the control condition than the experimental conditions, suggesting a floor effect. However, the general trend was for control writers to report fewer health visits and for exposure and writing paradigm writers to report slightly more health visits from prewriting to follow-up.

Health visits did not respond to exposure writing or the writing paradigm in the present study. However, the main dependent measures in the study involved trauma related variables such as PTSD symptoms and dissociation. Health was assessed in the present study by just one question regarding doctor visits, which is often utilized in writing paradigm studies as a convenient dependent measure.

Design Improvements in the Present Study

The present study contained several methodological changes that were meant to bolster the effectiveness of the writing paradigm by modifying the intervention to be more consistent with exposure-based treatments for PTSD. The first and most salient methodological modification was that SUDS were reported at five-minute intervals throughout the writing time. The second modification is that one condition was asked to write for 40 minutes, and was compared to the standard writing paradigm that asks participants in two conditions to write for 20 minutes about either a trauma or control topic. The third modification was asking those in the exposure condition to focus on sensory details related to the trauma, in an effort to increase exposure to trauma-related stimuli. The fourth modification was to utilize a sample that had experienced both a traumatic experience and PTSD symptoms that were consistent with DSM-IV criteria.

The primary alteration of the method resulted continuous reporting of SUDS, which was analyzed as a process variable. Consistent with hypothesis, SUDS scores tended to exhibit a quadratic relationship for the exposure and writing paradigm conditions, such that SUDS increased initially then decreased as writing time progressed. This finding is consistent with investigations involving Prolonged Exposure that indicate that individuals who experience a change in SUDS both within and between sessions tend to benefit the most from exposure (Foa & Kozak, 1986). More specifically, a general trend towards a decrease in SUDS was not found in the present study until approximately 25 minutes after writing, suggesting that lengthening the writing time may result in further decreases in SUDS. For the exposure condition, average SUDS was 19.9 at prewriting, 43.1 at minute 25 (highest mean), and 37.9 at postwriting. A total of 40 minutes of writing was utilized based on the findings of the present pilot study, which indicated that a writing time of 45 minutes may have been too physically taxing for participants. However, mean SUDS rating suggest that participants may have required more than 40 minutes of writing in order to experience a reduction in anxiety that approximated prewriting SUDS ratings.

Reporting SUDS also could have led to distraction from the writing task when participants were prompted every five minutes and asked to record SUDS score. A spoken auditory cue was also heard for several seconds prior to reporting, which could have compromised the writing task. Previous investigations involving Prolonged Exposure have found that difficulty maintaining attention to trauma-related stimuli during exposure can lead to decreased habituation (Foa & Kozak, 1986). Although in clinical contexts a therapist can ensure that the client focuses exclusively on the trauma, the present design included several opportunities for participants to be sidetracked by being prompted to be aware of SUDS, then reporting their score. One potential solution to this concern would be to ask that participants record SUDS after a brief non-verbal tone with their non-writing hand to minimize the distraction involved.

One other writing study has examined three specific SUDS ratings (average, highest, post-writing) that were reported after the writing task (Guastella & Dadds, 2006) rather than during writing. In this study, five writing conditions (control condition, writing paradigm condition, exposure condition, cognitive devaluation condition, and benefit-finding condition) wrote on three occasions and reported affect, panic, SUDS, and heart rate during each writing session. They found a significant main effect for condition and time, but not for an interaction. Post-hoc tests indicated that exposure, writing paradigm, and cognitive conditions reported higher average SUDS than benefit-finding and control conditions. Evidence for concurrent validity of SUDS and panic, as measured by the Body Sensation Questionnaire, was found by significant positive correlations during all three writing sessions. Only one significant condition difference for heart rate was found, which indicated that the exposure condition experienced higher heart rates during the first writing session. The presence of both main effects may indicate that although all conditions tend to habituate somewhat to their topic across sessions, conditions that focus on the negative aspects of trauma experience the most habituation (Guastella & Dadds, 2006).

The present study differed from the Guastella & Dadds (2006) study in several ways. First, the present study only examined three conditions whereas the latter study examined five. Second, SUDS scores from the present study were assessed several times during the writing task, as opposed to SUDS scores being reported retrospectively for the highest, average, and postwriting SUDS (Guastella & Dadds, 2006). Third, SUDS were found to correlate with symptoms of panic in the latter study but panic was not assessed in the present study. The present study appears to be unique in that no current published study has examined SUDS scores during and across writing sessions.

The second methodological change was that one condition was asked to write for 40 minutes, exactly double the writing time associated with most writing paradigm studies (Pennebaker, 2004). The present design did not yield any significant differences for those who wrote about trauma for 40 minutes versus those who wrote about trauma for 20 minutes. Analysis of SUDS scores did suggest that writing for 40 minutes may better attenuate participants to their subjective distress associated with the trauma compared to writing for 20 minutes. However, SUDS analysis also indicated that writing for an extended time, such as 50 minutes or more, may allow participants to more fully resolve the anxiety that they experience when writing about a trauma. Some empirically supported treatments for PTSD call for exposure session lengths of up to 75 minutes (Resick & Schnicke, 1992b) or 100 minutes (Keane et al., 1989). Therefore, examining writing about a trauma for 50 or more minutes may provide a more enhanced form of exposure and resulting decrease in PTSD symptoms.

The third methodological change was to request that those in the exposure writing condition focus on sensory details related to the trauma. This change was intended to enhance the quality of exposure, yet it was unsuccessful. Linguistic analysis failed to indicate a significant difference in word usage between the exposure and writing paradigm conditions for overall sensory words, hearing words, seeing words, or feeling words. Additional instructions, prompting, or training may be necessary for participants to utilize more trauma-related sensory information in their essays.

A fourth methodological change was to screen potential participants for a trauma history and current PTSD symptoms. Several writing studies have screened for a trauma history (Antal & Range, 2005; DeBrule & Range, 2005), yet many failed to exclude individuals who suffered from bereavement and other stressors rather than trauma (Deters & Range, 2003). The present screening form was an efficient means of gauging many aspects of reported traumas that are relevant to DSM-IV criteria. The present form also allowed for only those with significant PTSD symptoms to participate. A few writing studies have examined a sample screened for a trauma and symptoms consistent with DSM-IV criteria for PTSD (with significant PTSD symptoms. Although one preliminary study found that writing exacerbated PTSD symptoms in a small inpatient sample (Gidron et al., 1996), the present study is consistent with other investigations that have found writing is beneficial for participants with PTSD symptoms (Sloan et al., 2004) and somewhat beneficial for participants with a PTSD diagnosis (Smyth et al., 2008).

Methodological improvements in the present study, such as measuring SUDS and screening for PTSD were somewhat successful, whereas adjusting writing time and instructions for the exposure condition did not seem to affect outcomes. The findings for SUDS scores both within and across writing sessions are promising as they suggest that anxiety during writing tends to peak at 20-25 minutes and that further lengthening the writing session may result in a return to prewriting levels of anxiety. However, additional modifications and methodological changes are needed to make the basic writing paradigm more like a form of exposure. Present results and other writing studies tend to indicate that PTSD symptoms and other variables do not respond to the writing paradigm, which calls for the use of a more exposure based writing intervention than the writing paradigm. Future investigations should examine additional methodological permutations such as longer writing times, less intrusive methods of reporting SUDS, and other process variables related to exposure, such as heart rate, in order to enhance written exposure.

Natural Disaster and the Writing Paradigm

The present study was unique in that the writing paradigm and a written exposure task was implemented on a sample that was directly affected by a widespread natural disaster. The present study was conducted directly after Hurricane Katrina, which affected the present university as well as several metropolitan areas within 100 miles of the present university. All participants completed the present study within one year of Katrina, which was the most deadly hurricane since 1928 and most destructive natural disaster in American history, with an estimated total damage of over $100 billion dollars (Beven, et al., 2008).

Initial indications of the mental health effects of Katrina have reported prevalence rates for any DSM-IV anxiety disorder to be 49.1% among New Orleans residents and 26.4% among residents of all other Gulf Coast areas (Galea et al., 2007). The short-term effects of this specific natural disaster were not assessed in the present study. However, the screening procedure excluded many individuals who suffered from minor effects of Katrina ("our power was knocked out for a few days") and included several individuals who experienced threat to physical integrity of self or others, as well as fear, helplessness, or horror during Katrina ("I feared for my life"). Among those who qualified and participated, roughly one-third reported Katrina as a most severe or secondary trauma, and several participants in all three conditions wrote about Katrina directly or indirectly.

The present design may have been useful for those impacted by Katrina, yet writing about Katrina months after the incident may not have been ideal. One unresolved issue in the writing paradigm literature concerns the timing of the intervention respective to passage of time since the trauma. Initially, Pennebaker, Kiecolt-Glazer, & Glazer (1996) suggested that the writing paradigm is most appropriate for individuals who have resolved basic emotional and logistical issues that often accompany trauma, suggesting that the intervention may not amenable to participants who are still seeking basic needs in the aftermath of a hurricane. In contrast, one other study has examined the writing paradigm in the aftermath of a natural disaster such as a hurricane (Smyth, et al., 2002), yet this study only examined the relationship of intrusive thoughts, affect, and physical symptoms, rather than PTSD symptoms and dissociation. Writing led to diminished impact of intrusion on physical health diminished for trauma writers, but not for control writers (Smyth, et al., 2002), suggesting that the writing paradigm is a relatively safe intervention for survivors of a recent hurricane.

Another potential confound to the present study is that using writing as an exposure technique may be more appropriate for survivors of traumas other than a hurricane, such as assault. Exposure models suggest that fear elicitation is often strong for trauma-related cues of assault, which underlies the effect of treatment (Foa et al., 1991). Although the present participants suffered from a variety of traumas, those that wrote about Hurricane Katrina primarily focused on the effects and stressors related to the aftermath of the event rather than being afraid during the event. Also, the disinhibition model (Pennebaker, 1989) suggests that individuals may benefit most from a trauma that is rarely if ever discussed with others (e.g., victimization, incest) rather than traumas that are widely discussed among individuals and in mass media (e.g., natural disasters). Thus, writing may not have led to expected effects for some participants because many were consistently disclosing emotional and cognitive aspects about Katrina and being exposed to the disclosure of others.

Although it is difficult to directly assess the effect of Katrina on the present sample, the severity, duration, and scope of this particular trauma may have prevented responsiveness to a writing intervention for traumatic stress. One possibility specifically related to Katrina concerns the main effect of time noted for several dependent measures. Some participants may have experienced decreased PTSD symptoms and dissociation because of the mere passage of time and perhaps more adaptive coping to the trauma. Alternatively, some individuals in the present sample may have been experiencing problematic, stressful issues that have been associated with poor post-Katrina mental health, such as property loss, physical illness/injury, and other ongoing hurricane-related stressors (Galea et al., 2007). Therefore, at least some participants were probably experiencing significant stress related to the aftermath of the trauma, even during the course of participation. The use of writing as an early intervention for traumatic stress (e.g., Smyth et al., 2002) was not assessed in the present study, but present findings suggest that writing about a natural disaster may not be appropriate during the initial aftermath of the event.

Efficacy of Written Exposure

Present findings along with those from recent writing studies suggest that the writing paradigm in its current form may not yield sufficient exposure, and therefore, may not be a viable intervention for profound change in traumatic stress. The present protocol may have involved components of experimental writing in all three conditions, and each condition improved somewhat after writing, yet exposure writing failed to confer additional benefits. Writing about a trauma for 20 minutes has failed to yield better improvement in overall PTSD symptoms when compared to writing about a control topic for 20 minutes in several studies (DeBrule & Range, 2005; Deters & Range, 2003; Brown & Heimberg, 2001), with many of these studies finding no significant change in PTSD symptoms from prewriting to postwriting. The present study did not administer dependent measures postwriting, which may have indicated significant condition differences that existed briefly after writing yet disappeared by follow-up. For example, some studies have found benefits for reactivity to trauma briefly after a lengthy writing session (Smyth et al., 2008). Future writing studies should consider utilizing outcome assessment briefly after writing to better understand symptom change, while being careful to eliminate negative mood or anxiety associated with writing (Pennebaker & Francis, 1996) prior to the assessment.

Although many writing studies have exhibited limited efficaciousness for PTSD, there have been a few studies that have found expected effects for PTSD, depression, and health. Many of these studies report writing on either consecutive days (Sloan & Marx, 2004; Sloan et al., 2005) or several writing sessions on one day (Smyth et al., 2007).

Writing studies that have found benefits exclusively among trauma writers have also found large to medium effect sizes for numerous measures of PTSD, mood, and health among treatment-seeking women who suffered a sexual assault (Sloan & Marx, 2004; Sloan et al., 2005) or men who involved in combat. Thus, more recent, tightly controlled studies have found promising effects for treatment-seeking survivors of specific traumas.

Present SUDS ratings indicate that written exposure may require a lengthy writing time. Writing about a trauma for merely 20 minutes typically resulted in escalating SUDS levels, but writing for 40 minutes about a trauma resulted in an initial escalation in SUDS with a gradual decrease starting at approximately 25 minutes into writing. This process finding may help explain the lack of effect found in several writing paradigm studies that have used trauma samples. The theoretical basis for both prolonged exposure (Jaycox et al., 1998) and flooding (Lyons & Keane, 1989) calls for the individual to experience an initial increase then a decrease in SUDS for maximal effectiveness. Furthermore, allowing the individual to stop an exposure session when SUDS are the highest may be counterproductive as it "might strengthen the patients' belief that the trauma is too horrible to manage" (Lyons & Keane, 1989, p. 147). Thus, individuals who write for 20 minutes that report the highest SUDS at postwriting may not benefit from exposure as much as individuals who write for 40 minutes that report an initial increase then decrease in SUDS towards the end of the writing time.

Writing as a form of exposure may not be sufficient for long-term change in PTSD symptoms, yet exposure-based writing does lead to similar short-term improvement when compared to empirically supported treatments such as EMDR

(Lango-Marsh & Spates, 2002) and CPT (Resick et al., 2008). A recent dismantling study of cognitive processing therapy sought to find differential effects for the entire 12 session treatment, six sessions of written exposure alone, or six sessions of cognitive restructuring alone (Resick et al., 2008). All three conditions reported initial improvement in symptoms of PTSD and depression, but the writing alone condition tended to report less improvement than the cognitive alone condition as treatment progressed. The superior performance of cognitive therapy alone without any formal exposure task suggests that addressing multiple trauma-related cognitions can be slightly more effective than exposure in sexual assault victims. However, several caveats were noted, including the lack of standard writing instructions, lack of external validity for survivors of other traumas, and limited power (Resick et al., 2008). The main clinical implications were that the cognitive portion of CPT may be the most favorable choice for clients who dislike exposure or can only attend a limited number of sessions, and the written exposure portion of CPT may be best for therapists who serve large rural populations or lack expertise with cognitive therapy (Resick et al., 2008).

The beneficial effect for written exposure found in the CPT dismantling study (Resick et al., 2008) also suggests that interpersonal contact regarding the writing may enhance effect. Empirical evidence for this notion has been suggested in other studies. In one study, an additional effect of increased insight and effort were noted in those that interacted with a warm versus cold experimenter during the writing paradigm, although no change occurred for dependent measures (Rogers, Wilson, Gohm, & Merwin, 2007). It may be that some of the benefits of the writing paradigm may be partially due to disclosing a severe trauma in the presence of a supportive individual, as well as the cognitive processing associated with answering questionnaires before intervention. Writing alone for six sessions was sufficient as a stand alone treatment for PTSD, leading to immediate significant effects on PTSD symptoms (Resick et al., 2008). However, additional interventions, such as sessions of cognitive therapy, may be necessary to prolong benefits.

The efficacy of written exposure remains unclear. Recent writing paradigm investigations have exhibited a trend towards finding benefits exclusively for trauma writers, yet these investigations are outnumbered by studies that have failed to find condition differences. Studies that have adapted their intervention from the writing paradigm or other PTSD treatments have tended to support hypothesis. Thus, future investigations that expand on the writing paradigm or adapt a pre-existing protocol for exposure may be the most likely to exhibit a large effect.

Future Research

The present design included several methodological changes to the standard writing paradigm, such as adding a condition that wrote for an adjusted writing time and received instructions based on exposure models. Although the primary hypothesis of the study was not supported, the use of an exposure condition did reveal significant aspects of how the writing paradigm may differ from exposure-based written interventions. Also, present dependent measures may have been complemented by additional measures of psychological and physical health. Finally, use of SUDS as a process variable was a unique and useful aspect of the present design. Future writing studies that examine PTSD in trauma survivors should focus on adjusting or expanding four content areas: writing time and number of sessions, writing topic, dependent measures, and process variables.

One methodological improvement that future studies should consider is improving exposure by lengthening writing time and utilizing additional days of writing. The protocol for Prolonged Exposure calls for six or more spoken exposure sessions (Foa & Meadows, 1997), and CPT calls for a minimum of two 75-minute written exposure sessions along with daily reading of the written trauma account across two weeks (Resick et al., 2008). No writing paradigm study has utilized more than four sessions or a writing time of more than 30 minutes, yet one study that lacked a control condition did find that three 60- minute sessions of trauma writing led to improvement similar to EMDR (Lango-Marsh & Spates, 2005). Although the present design did aim to create an exposure condition for writing by doubling the amount of time, further increases in writing time may be needed to confer additional benefits. Present SUDS ratings did suggest that writing for 60 minutes or more could result in further decreases in anxiety, and other investigations have found promising results for a six-session writing protocol (Resick et al., 2008).

An alternative method that is consistent with exposure protocols could involve utilizing SUDS as an indication of when to stop the writing session, rather than time. Participants could be asked to write continuously and report SUDS throughout writing, and experimenters could determine the end of the writing session relative to the elicitation and reduction in SUDS. Exposure protocols often call for a significant increase in SUDS (from 50 to 70) during a session, and generally estimate that 90 to 120 minutes

of time will be needed for SUDS to decrease back to baseline (Foa & Kozak, 1986).
Future studies should consider lengthening the writing time or utilizing a measure of
anxiety as a means of determining the ideal length of each writing session.

Present results also suggest that additional writing days may be necessary because
the last (Day 4) writing session was significantly different from other days of writing. On
Day 4, all participants tended to report fewer positive emotion words, negative emotion
words, and cognitive mechanism words, yet more insight words compared to all other
days of writing. This trend was more prominent for specific LIWC counts, such that
approximately six times as many negative words were used from Day 3 compared to Day
4, and approximately six times less insight words were used from Day 3 compared to Day
4. This indicates that participants may have utilized the final day of writing for reflection
and summarizing their work, rather than as a final session of exposure. One potential
solution to this trend would be to implement a warm-up writing session and provide
additional writing sessions given that the final essay may be used for summary and
closure. Future studies should examine if a protocol with six or more sessions involving
more than 40 minutes of writing time (e.g., Resick et al., 2008) may be more
advantageous than the standard writing paradigm.

A second methodological consideration is the appropriateness of an exposure-
based writing topic. Present instructions requested that exposure writers focus on sensory
information related to trauma, but these instructions did not lead to condition differences
in word usage. However, other writing paradigm investigations have found that adjusting
the writing topic to focus on emotional processing led to fewer PTSD symptoms and

better health when compared to a cognitive topic and control topic (Sloan, Marx, Epstein, & Lexington, 2007). Furthermore, other studies have found either significant improvement in PTSD symptoms for altering topics between six weekly writing sessions (Resick et al., 2008) or no improvement for PTSD symptoms for a one-time intervention with three different writing topics (Smyth et al., 2008). One consistent outcome of investigations that alter the instructions of the writing paradigm is less physiological reactivity to the trauma in terms of heart rate (Sloan et al., 2007) and salivary cortisol (Smyth, et al., 2008).

Although several studies have sought to examine unique writing topic adjustments for PTSD symptoms, no specific exposure writing protocol has been established. One potential writing topic adjustment that would be more consistent with exposure models would be to establish a hierarchy of trauma-related events (Foa & Kozak, 1986) then request that participants write about increasingly difficult aspects of one trauma across sessions. Implementing a hierarchy could clarify the rationale and writing content necessary for exposure, and ensure that writing results in a high amount of SUDS, which has been identified as a beneficial aspect of exposure (Foa et al., 1991). Although mean SUDS were fairly high for present exposure writers on Day 1, mean SUDS for Days 2-4 did not exceed 50, suggesting that more specific writing instructions may have been necessary to elicit a sufficiently high SUDS for exposure to be effective. Future studies should consider use of additional instructions that provide better guidance for exposure writing and/or altering writing topics to include other common aspects of exposure treatment, such as a fear hierarchy.

A third methodological aspect for future investigation involves the use of several dependent measures for outcomes related to trauma, mood, and health. Writing paradigm studies have found large effect sizes for measures such as salivary cortisol, the Posttraumatic Diagnostic Scale, the Beck Depression Inventory-II, and the Pennebaker Inventory of Limbic Languidness (Sloan & Marx, 2004). The present study and studies at the present university (DeBrule & Range, 2005; Deters & Range, 2003) have failed to detect condition differences for the total score of the IES-R, although several studies have reported strong psychometric properties for the IES-R (Creamer et al., 2003). The present study also failed to detect condition differences for self-reported health visits, consistent with other studies at the present university (DeBrule & Range, 2005; Deters & Range, 2003; Kovac & Range, 2000; Range et al., 2000). However, writing studies have tended to find benefits for specific health measures, suggesting that future studies should consider use of health measures that are particularly relevant to a given sample. Future studies should utilize numerous dependent measures in order to detect the effect of writing on general and specific areas of mental and physical health.

A fourth methodological consideration is the assessment of process variables that may explain the presence or absence of effect. In the present study, SUDS were utilized as a basic inexpensive process variable, yet other measures that require equipment such as heart rate, blood pressure, and cortisol were not assessed. Only one writing study has examined both heart rate and SUDS as process variables, but failed to assess heart rate because of equipment failure and failed to assess SUDS continuously throughout the writing task (Guastella & Dadds, 2006). Heart rate was assessed as a measure of psychophysiological reactivity to trauma in another recent study (Sloan et al., 2007). Continuous measures of heart rate indicated that writing about emotions related to trauma was associated with better habituation to trauma compared to writing about cognitions related to trauma or a control topic (Sloan et al., 2007). Although two writing studies have assessed anxiety or reactivity through SUDS and heart rate, no writing study has examined the potential moderating or mediating effect of anxiety ratings or psychophysiological measures during writing. Additional moderators such as optimism and alexithymia have been found to significantly affect the outcome of writing on dependent measures (Balkie, 2008), yet few writing studies assess personality. Future research should examine how writing interventions affect numerous process related variables, such as SUDS, heart rate, blood pressure, and salivary cortisol, and examine how these variables and other aspects of personality.

The present protocol failed to provide a paradigm for exposure-based writing, but did include some significant design improvements and errors that should be considered by future studies. Exposure may be further enhanced by writing for more than 40 minutes about varying topics, in contrast to present exposure writing for 40 minutes about the same topic. The exclusive effects of exposure writing may also become clearer through further assessment of multiple trauma-related outcome measures, general measures of psychological health, and the potential influence of process variables such as SUDS (Guastella & Dadds, 2006), heart rate (Sloan et al., 2007), and alexythymia (Balkie, 2008; Paez, Velasco, & Gonzales, 1999). Present findings may provide a point of departure for future writing paradigm and written exposure investigations as a framework for comparing these interventions. Design modifications that expand on present modifications appear to be necessary to create an efficacious exposure-based writing protocol that results in more benefits than the writing paradigm.

The present study failed to confirm the primary hypothesis that exposure writing would result in less PTSD symptoms, dissociation, and health visits from prewriting to follow-up compared to the writing paradigm and control writing. However, the present study did indicate that PTSD symptoms and dissociation improved for all three writing conditions across time in a sample that was screened for trauma and symptoms of PTSD. This unexpected pattern of results could have been due to unintended exposure in the control condition, insufficient exposure in the exposure condition, and a lack of power following attrition. Health visits may not have responded whatsoever to the current protocol because all conditions engaged in some emotional expression, although use of a more thorough questionnaire and/or a specific health variable could have been a more sensitive measure of health.

Conclusions of the present study are limited and tentative at best because of methodological errors, the effect of a severe hurricane, and the atypical design that was utilized. Linguistic analysis and essay ratings provided a manipulation check that indicated participants followed directions, yet some essay ratings suggested that all conditions wrote about a profound topic. Exposure writing instructions did not result in significant linguistic changes, and may not have resulted in significant changes in dependent measures because participants did not have enough time to continue to report decreases in anxiety. Hurricane Katrina may have inadvertently affected results because many respondents denied participation on the screening form, some participants in the control condition wrote about Katrina-related stress, and some participants may have been experiencing current distress associated with the aftermath of the hurricane. The present design utilized a third condition in addition to the writing paradigm, and involved specific design changes that are not typical of the writing paradigm, such as SUDS reporting. Therefore, present findings are cautionary because of uniqueness of both the sample and design.

Factors unique to the present study call for replication of the present design, and additional writing paradigm studies may indicate the efficacy of this widely researched protocol. In addition, present findings and similar writing investigations have tended to find beneficial yet unclear effects for PTSD symptoms. Investigations that reported the strongest effects tended to be those that involved an innovative method that altered writing time or topic, and those that assessed several areas of psychological and physical health. The most innovative and successful aspect of the present design was that SUDS ratings exhibited an anticipated quadratic trend for the exposure condition. Future research should utilize SUDS ratings and focus on further refining an exposure writing protocol by examining various writing times, writing topics, process variables, and dependent measures.

Further studies are necessary to better determine the efficacy of various written exposure protocols and the writing paradigm. Few studies have examined either the writing paradigm or a stand-alone writing treatment in a screened trauma sample with PTSD symptoms, either as the writing paradigm (Sloan & Marx, 2004) or as a modified version of the writing paradigm (Smyth et al., 2008; Sloan et al., 2007) or CPT (Resick et al., 2008). However, writing paradigm studies examining various outcomes have substantially increased across the past 10 years. An initial meta-analysis reported a total of 13 writing paradigm studies that met inclusion (Smyth, 1998), yet a recent meta-analysis that analyzed the health outcomes in 30 writing paradigm studies reported that over 100 writing paradigm studies have been conducted (Harris, 2006). Numerous investigations that involved a novel written exposure task have also emerged recently (Resick et al., 2008; Smyth et al., 2007). A substantial number of experimental studies and meta-analysis may be necessary to fully understand how exposure-based writing protocols and the standard writing paradigm affect PTSD symptoms, dissociation, and physical health.

APPENDIX A
TRAUMA HISTORY SCREEN (CARLSON, 2000)

The events below may or may not have happened to you. Circle "YES" if that kind of thing has happened to you or circle "NO" if that kind of thing has not happened to you. **If you circle "YES" for any events:** put a number in the blank next to it to show how many times something like that happened.

**Number of times
Something like this happened**

A. A really bad car, boat, train, or airplane accident	NO	YES	_____
B. A really bad accident at work or home	NO	YES	_____
C. A hurricane, flood, earthquake, tornado, or fire	NO	YES	_____
D. Getting beat up or attacked – as a child	NO	YES	_____
E. Getting beat up or attacked – as an adult	NO	YES	_____
F. Forced sex – as a child	NO	YES	_____
G. Forced sex – as an adult	NO	YES	_____
H. Attack with a gun, knife, or weapon	NO	YES	_____
I. During military service – seeing something horrible or being badly scared	NO	YES	_____
J. Sudden death of close family or friend	NO	YES	_____
K. Seeing someone badly hurt or killed	NO	YES	_____
L. Some other event that scared you badly	NO	YES	_____

Did any of these things really bother you emotionally? NO YES
If you answered "YES", fill out a box to tell about EVERY event that really bothered you.
There are more boxes on the other side of the pages.

Letter from above for the type of event: _____   Your age when this happened: ____ Describe what happened: When this happened, did anyone get hurt or killed?   NO   YES When this happened, were you afraid that you or someone else might get hurt or killed?   NO   YES When this happened, did you feel very afraid, helpless, or horrified?   NO   YES When this happened, did you feel unreal, spaced out, disoriented, or strange? NO   YES After this happened, how long were you bothered by it? Not at all / 1 week / 2-3 weeks / a month or more At that time, how much were you bothered emotionally? Not at all / 1 week / 2-3 weeks / a month or more

Letter from above for the type of event: _____   Your age when this happened: ____ Describe what happened: When this happened, did anyone get hurt or killed?   NO   YES When this happened, were you afraid that you or someone else might get hurt or killed?   NO   YES When this happened, did you feel very afraid, helpless, or horrified?   NO   YES When this happened, did you feel unreal, spaced out, disoriented, or strange? NO   YES After this happened, how long were you bothered by it? Not at all / 1 week / 2-3 weeks / a month or more At that time, how much were you bothered emotionally? Not at all / 1 week / 2-3 weeks / a month or more

Letter from above for the type of event: _____   Your age when this happened: _____
Describe what happened:

When this happened, did anyone get hurt or killed?   NO   YES
When this happened, were you afraid that you
or someone else might get hurt or killed?   NO   YES
When this happened, did you feel very afraid, helpless, or horrified?   NO   YES
When this happened, did you feel unreal, spaced out, disoriented, or strange? NO   YES
After this happened, how long were you bothered by it? Not at all / 1 week / 2-3 weeks / a month or more
At that time, how much were you bothered emotionally? Not at all / 1 week / 2-3 weeks / a month or more

---

Letter from above for the type of event: _____   Your age when this happened: _____
Describe what happened:

When this happened, did anyone get hurt or killed?   NO   YES
When this happened, were you afraid that you
or someone else might get hurt or killed?   NO   YES
When this happened, did you feel very afraid, helpless, or horrified?   NO   YES
When this happened, did you feel unreal, spaced out, disoriented, or strange? NO   YES
After this happened, how long were you bothered by it? Not at all / 1 week / 2-3 weeks / a month or more
At that time, how much were you bothered emotionally? Not at all / 1 week / 2-3 weeks / a month or more

---

Letter from above for the type of event: _____   Your age when this happened: _____
Describe what happened:

When this happened, did anyone get hurt or killed?   NO   YES
When this happened, were you afraid that you
or someone else might get hurt or killed?   NO   YES
When this happened, did you feel very afraid, helpless, or horrified?   NO   YES
When this happened, did you feel unreal, spaced out, disoriented, or strange? NO   YES
After this happened, how long were you bothered by it? Not at all / 1 week / 2-3 weeks / a month or more
At that time, how much were you bothered emotionally? Not at all / 1 week / 2-3 weeks / a month or more

---

Letter from above for the type of event: _____   Your age when this happened: _____
Describe what happened:

When this happened, did anyone get hurt or killed?   NO   YES
When this happened, were you afraid that you
or someone else might get hurt or killed?   NO   YES
When this happened, did you feel very afraid, helpless, or horrified?   NO   YES
When this happened, did you feel unreal, spaced out, disoriented, or strange? NO   YES
After this happened, how long were you bothered by it? Not at all / 1 week / 2-3 weeks / a month or more
At that time, how much were you bothered emotionally? Not at all / 1 week / 2-3 weeks / a month or more

APPENDIX B
CONTACT QUESTIONNAIRE

Are you interested in a research study involving trauma?

YES   **NO**

If you are interested, please provide the following information

Name:_____

Phone Number:_____

Cellular Phone Number:_____

Email Address:_____

What was the most severe trauma you experienced?

How long ago did the most severe trauma happen?

Are you taking medication or seeking treatment for any mental illness at the present time?

APPENDIX C
SCREEN FOR POSTTRAUMATIC STRESS SYMPTOMS (SPTSS)

IN THE BLANK SPACE BEFORE EACH QUESTION, PUT A NUMBER TO TELL HOW MUCH THAT THING HAS HAPPENED TO YOU *IN THE PAST WEEK.*

0 = not at all

1 = 1 or 2 times

2 = almost every day

3 = at least once every day

4 = more than once every day

___1. I don't feel like doing things that I used to like doing.

___2. I can't remember much about the bad things that have happened to me.

___3. I feel cut off and isolated from other people.

___4. I try not to think about things that remind me of something bad that happened to me.

___5. I feel numb: I don't feel emotions as strongly as I used to.

___6. I have trouble concentrating on things or paying attention to something for a long time.

___7. I have a hard time thinking about the future and believing that I'm going to live to old age.

___8. I feel very irritable and lose my temper.

___9. I avoid doing things or being in situations that might remind me of something terrible that happened to me in the past.

___10. I am very aware of my surroundings and nervous about what's going on around me.

___11. I find myself remembering bad things that happened to me over and over, even when I don't want to think about them.

___12. I get startled or surprised very easily and "jump" when I hear a sudden sound.

___13. I have bad dreams about terrible things that happened to me.

___14. I get very upset when something reminds me of something bad that happened to me.

___15. I have trouble getting to sleep or staying asleep.

___16. When something reminds me of something bad that happened to me, I feel shaky, sweaty, nervous, and my heart beats really fast.

___17. I suddenly feel like I am back in the past, in a bad satiation that I was once in, and it's like it was happening all over again.

APPENDIX D
DEMOGRAPHIC QUESTIONNAIRE

1. GENDER: Female_____   Male_____

2. AGE: _____

3. RACE: African-American _____   Hispanic _____
          Asian _____   Native American _____
          Caucasian _____   Other:_____

4. YEAR IN COLLEGE: Freshman _____   Senior _____
                     Sophomore _____   Other _____
                     Junior _____

5. How many times have you visited the health center, school clinic, or family doctor, in the past two months? _____

6. List the most traumatic experience that you have gone through in brief detail. If you have suffered from two or more traumatic experiences, please describe them as well.

7. The most traumatic event I experienced is **(Please describe only one trauma that was the worst):**

   _____
   _____
   _____
   _____

8. I experienced other traumatic events, such as:

   _____
   _____
   _____
   _____

9. The most traumatic event occurred on this date: / /   Today's date: / /

10. On a scale of 1 (No threat) to 10 (An extreme amount), how much did you think that your life was in danger? _____

11. The most severe trauma I experienced lasted for this long:_____

APPENDIX E
ESSAY EVALUATION FORM

The following questions pertain to the essay that you have just written. Please answer these questions as honestly as possible.

	Not at all						A great Deal
1. How personal was your essay?	1	2	3	4	5	6	7
2. How meaningful was your essay?	1	2	3	4	5	6	7
3. How severe was the event described in your essay?	1	2	3	4	5	6	7
4. How revealing of emotion was your essay?	1	2	3	4	5	6	7
5. How much is the topic described in your essay still affecting your life?	1	2	3	4	5	6	7
6. how much have you talked with others about the topic?	1	2	3	4	5	6	7
7. How much have you wanted to talk to others about the topic?	1	2	3	4	5	6	7
8. How much have you actively held back from talking to others about the topic?	1	2	3	4	5	6	7

9. Do you expect this writing exercise to have some benefit? YES or NO

10. If you are upset enough that you need to be contacted right away, check this box.

APPENDIX F
IMPACT OF EVENT SCALE – REVISED (IES-R)

Instructions: Then following is a list of difficulties people sometimes have after stressful life events. Please read each item, and then indicate how distressing each difficulty has been for you during the past 7 days, with respect to the very stressful and traumatic event that you experienced. How much were you distressed or bothered by these difficulties?

0=Not at all   1=A little bit   2=Moderately   3=Quite a bit   4=Extremely

1. Any reminder brought back feelings about it.	0	1	2	3	4
2. I had trouble staying asleep.	0	1	2	3	4
3. Other things kept making me think about it.	0	1	2	3	4
4. I felt irritable and angry.	0	1	2	3	4
5. I avoided letting myself get upset when I thought about it or was reminded of it.	0	1	2	3	4
6. I thought about it when I didn't mean to.	0	1	2	3	4
7. I felt as if it hadn't happened or wasn't real.	0	1	2	3	4
8. I stayed away from reminders about it.	0	1	2	3	4
9. Pictures about it popped into my mind.	0	1	2	3	4
10. I was jumpy and easily startled.	0	1	2	3	4
11. I tried not to think about it.	0	1	2	3	4
12. I was aware that I still had a lot of feelings about it, but I didn't deal with them.	0	1	2	3	4
13. My feelings about it were kind of numb.	0	1	2	3	4
14. I found myself acting or feeling like I was back at that time.	0	1	2	3	4
15. I had trouble falling asleep.	0	1	2	3	4
16. I had waves of strong feelings about it.	0	1	2	3	4
17. I tried to remove it from my memory.	0	1	2	3	4
18. I had trouble concentrating.	0	1	2	3	4
19. Reminders of it caused me to have physical reactions, such as sweating, trouble breathing, nausea, or a pounding heart.	0	1	2	3	4
20. I had dreams about it.	0	1	2	3	4
21. I felt watchful and on guard.	0	1	2	3	4
22. I tried not to talk about it.	0	1	2	3	4

APPENDIX G
POSTTRAUMATIC DISSOCIATION SCALE (PTD, CARLSON & WAELDE, 2000)
For each statement below, circle one of the choices to show how many times each thing has happened to you in the past week.

	NOT ONCE	ONCE, TWICE	THREE TO SIX	SEVEN TO 10	MORE than 10
1. My body felt strange or unreal	0	1-2	3-6	7-10	10+
2. Things around me seemed strange or unreal.	0	1-2	3-6	7-10	10+
3. I got reminded of something upsetting then spaced out for a while.	0	1-2	3-6	7-10	10+
4. I had moments when I lost control and acted like I was back in an upsetting time in my past.	0	1-2	3-6	7-10	10+
5. I noticed that I couldn't remember the details of something upsetting that happened to me.	0	1-2	3-6	7-10	10+
6. Familiar places seemed strange or unreal.	0	1-2	3-6	7-10	10+
7. I felt like I was outside myself, watching myself do things.	0	1-2	3-6	7-10	10+
8. I heard something that I know really wasn't there.	0	1-2	3-6	7-10	10+
9. I got upset about something and can't get over it.	0	1-2	3-6	7-10	10+
10. I felt like I was in a movie – like nothing that was happening was real.	0	1-2	3-6	7-10	10+
11. I didn't feel pain when I was hurt and should have felt something.	0	1-2	3-6	7-10	10+
12. A memory came back to me that was so strong that I lost track of what was going on around me.	0	1-2	3-6	7-10	10+
13. I found myself staring into space and thinking of nothing.	0	1-2	3-6	7-10	10+
14. I couldn't remember things that had happened during the day even when I tried to.	0	1-2	3-6	7-10	10+
15. I felt like I wasn't myself.	0	1-2	3-6	7-10	10+
16. I felt like I was in a daze and couldn't make sense of what was going on around me.	0	1-2	3-6	7-10	10+
17. I saw something that seemed real, but was not.	0	1-2	3-6	7-10	10+
18. I suddenly realized that I hadn't been paying attention to what was going on around me.	0	1-2	3-6	7-10	10+
19. I felt cut off from what was going on around me.	0	1-2	3-6	7-10	10+
20. Parts of my body seemed distorted – like they were bigger or smaller than usual.	0	1-2	3-6	7-10	10+
21. I reacted to people or situations as if I were back in an upsetting time in my past.	0	1-2	3-6	7-10	10+
22. I got so focused on something going on in my mind that I lost track of what was happening around me.	0	1-2	3-6	7-10	10+
23. I noticed there were gaps in my memory for things that happened to me that I should be able to remember.	0	1-2	3-6	7-10	10+
24. I smelled something I know really wasn't there.	0	1-2	3-6	7-10	10+

APPENDIX H

PTSD CHECKLIST – CIVILIAN VERSION (PCL-C)

INSTRUCTIONS: Below is a list of problems and complaints that people sometimes have in response to stressful life experiences. Please read each one carefully and indicate how much you have been bothered by that problem **in the past month**.

1. Not at all   **2.** A little bit   3. Moderately   **4.** Quite a bit   **5.** Extremely

1. Repeated disturbing MEMORIES, THOUGHTS, or IMAGES of the stressful experience from the past ?	1	2	3	4	5
2. Repeated disturbing DREAMS of the stressful experience from the past?	1	2	3	4	5
3. Suddenly ACTING or FEELING as if the stressful experience from the past were happening again (as if you were reliving it)?	1	2	3	4	5
4. Feeling VERY UPSET when SOMETHING reminded you of the stressful experience from the past?	1	2	3	4	5
5. Having PHYSICAL reactions (e.g. heart pounding, trouble breathing, sweating) when SOMETHING REMINDED you of the stressful experience from the past?	1	2	3	4	5
6. Avoiding THINKING ABOUT or TALKING ABOUT the stressful experience from the past or AVOIDING HAVING FEELINGS related to it?	1	2	3	4	5
7. Avoiding ACTIVITIES or SITUATIONS because they REMINDED you of the stressful experience from the past?	1	2	3	4	5
8. Feeling EMOTIONALLY NUMB or being unable to have loving feelings for those close to you?	1	2	3	4	5
9. Trouble FALLING or STAYING ASLEEP?	1	2	3	4	5
10. Feeling IRRITABLE or having ANGRY OUTBURST?	1	2	3	4	5
11. Having DIFFICULTY CONCENTRATING?	1	2	3	4	5
12. Being "SUPER ALERT" or watchful or on guard?	1	2	3	4	5
13. Feeling JUMPY or easily startled?	1	2	3	4	5
14. Trouble REMEMBERING IMPORTANT PARTS of the stressful experience form the past?	1	2	3	4	5
15. LOSS OF INTEREST in activities that you used to enjoy?	1	2	3	4	5
16. Feeling as if your FUTURE somehow will be CUT SHORT?	1	2	3	4	5
17. Feeling DISTANT OR CUT OFF from people?	1	2	3	4	5

APPENDIX I

INSTRUCTIONS FOR DATA ANALYSIS WITH THE SLIWC PROGRAM

For use with PC with Microsoft Word© 2000, SPSS© - version 10, & Windows NT

1. To purchase SLIWC, contact James W. Pennebaker, Department of Psychology, The University of Texas at Austin, Austin, Texas, 78712, (512) – 232-2781.
2. Make sure all files are saved separately in text (.txt) format.
3. Process for saving text files appropriate for LIWC analysis
   a. Make sure that successive periods do not occur in the sample.
   b. Take out all periods that do not end a sentence (6:30p.m. = 6:30pm).
   c. Remove all dashes.
   d. Correct all spelling errors.
   e. Make any other necessary adjustments to writing sample for text analysis
4. Save file in eight characters - Code name or identification number in first five characters, then code file for group with the sixth character and seventh character, then for day with the eighth character. (i.e. - John Doe's writing sample for day 2 in the trauma group would be coded as JohndTr2).
5. To load software, go to run, then type A:/WLIWC/Run or click on LIWC icon.
6. Go to File on the LIWC window, then Process, then Browse for Input File.
7. From your directory, select the file folder that contains text files for input, then any specific text file.
8. Click OK.
9. Click on the file name next to Browse and change the last character of the file name from 1,2,3, or 4 to a "?" to process all files (written samples) for a given individual (i.e. "johndrt2" becomes "johndtr?").
10. Click on the Browse icon directly next to the Output File Box.
11. Choose a file directory (i.e. My Documents) for the output file for the LIWC analysis.
12. Click OK.
13. Click OK again in the Files to Process Window.
14. SLIWC will indicate if all files were processed or if there was an error.
    a. If there is an error, recheck text files for periods, dashes, and remove.
15. Open SPSS.
16. Click on file, then open, then other.
17. Find the LIWC output file or icon in the directory you specified in Step11.
18. Open the file "LIWC – SPSS Syntax Editor".
19. Highlight each writing sample as a row, excluding the first line. Click on copy.
20. Paste data into SPSS by clicking on a case in the first column.
21. If conducting repeated measures analysis, place scores for all days of writing in the same row for each subject.
22. Close "LIWC – SPSS Syntax Editor".
23. Save database for LIWC Word Counts.
24. Repeat process with another participant, until database includes all cases. Label Column 1 in spreadsheet as Code name or Number, then label for each dependent measure given by the WLIC in columns 2-65. Fill in columns for grouping variables.

APPENDIX J
INFORMED CONSENT

UNIVERSITY OF SOUTHERN MISSISSIPPI
Informed Consent Document for Research Participants
Writing About the Past, Present, and Future

This research project is for a doctoral dissertation to assess the effects of writing about different personal topics on psychological and physical health. The writing topics may include personally sensitive material. Some examples of possible writing topics include writing about a traumatic experience you have gone through, such as a severe injury or personal attack, as well as more general topics. You will be asked to come to four meetings (Monday-Wednesdays, Tuesday-Thursdays, or Wednesdays-Fridays), the first meeting will take approximately 90 minutes, then the next three meetings will take 60 minutes. There are several writing groups in the study, and you will be randomly assigned to one of the writing groups. During each of the meetings, you will write about a topic given to you for twenty minutes, have the option to take a five minute break, and then write for twenty additional minutes. You will also complete a few questionnaires before and after the four weeks of writing. You will not place your name on your writings and only the main experimenters will read the writings, therefore, what you write will be anonymous and confidential. The only way you will identify yourself in the study will be through a codename that you select. Please make sure that your codename is unique and has not been used before (for grade postings, for example), and the confidentiality and anonymity of yourself and your peers will be preserved. You will be given the option of writing on paper or on computer. If you choose to write on paper, and you will seal your written work in an envelope and place them in a locked box. If you feel more comfortable using a computer, you will be allowed to type your topic on a laptop or PC instead of writing by hand. You will then store your writings on a computer disk provided to you, which you will seal in an envelope and place in a locked box after you finish. About six weeks after the last meeting, I will ask you to come in and complete some questionnaires that will take you about 20 minutes to complete. This study will thus consist of a 90-minute first session, three 60-minute sessions, and one final 30-minute session. For completing this study, you will be awarded at least 10 Experimetrix credits, which will count towards either extra credit or required research credit, as detailed by the instructor of your psychology course. For the sake of your peers who require research credit and the integrity of the study, please participate only if you are willing to attend all writing sessions.

Your participation is voluntary. You may discontinue at any time without penalty or prejudice. You will be asked to provide a nickname or code name, known only to you, to put on your forms. No personal names will be on the forms. All of the questionnaires and writings will be kept in a secure location and will be destroyed completely a few years after the completion of the study.

Your confidentiality throughout the study is important. During the study, your writings will be read by a clinical psychology graduate student who is the primary researcher, in order to ensure your safety and the safety of others. Your identity will be kept confidential unless you indicate in any of your writings or verbally that you have a current intent to harm yourself or someone else. If either of these should occur, your code will be matched with your name and confidentiality may be broken. A Clinical Psychologist who is supervising the study and I will meet with you to determine the best course of action for your safety. Based on previous studies conducted similar to this one, the risk of this occurring is very small.

It is likely that participation in this study will not directly benefit you. You will be compensated for taking the time to participate in the study through extra credit. You will receive extra credit for each writing session and for completing the questionnaires six weeks later. You will receive one and a half hours (3 credits) of research or extra credit for the first session, one hour of credit for the next three sessions (2 credits each day) and one-half hour of credit for completing the questionnaires on the final session. The Experimetrix points will be credited to your Experimetrix account after completing each writing session, the extra credit will be given to you. Should you decide to discontinue the study before it ends, you will receive extra credit for the amount of time you spent in the study. Please note that there will be several other opportunities for earning extra credit that are at your psychology's instructor's discretion; such as summarizing a professional article, attending a research presentation outside of class, and attending a psychology colloquium outside of class.

One of the risks of participating in the study is that you may experience a negative mood or sadness while writing or immediately after writing. Another risk is that you may experience somewhat more traumatic memories for a short time during the study. I will provide you with a handout of phone numbers of counseling services that you may contact in case you become upset at any time during this experiment. Should you feel upset or distressed in any way during the study, I will personally meet with you to provide appropriate referrals to mental health care providers who can meet your needs.

Consent is hereby given to participate in the research project entitled Writing about the past, present, and future. All experimental procedures were explained by Daniel DeBrule. Information was given about the risks, inconveniences, or discomforts that might be expected.

The opportunity to ask questions regarding the research and procedures was given. Participation in the project is completely voluntary and participants may withdraw at any time without penalty, prejudice, or loss of benefits. All personal information is strictly confidential and no names will be disclosed, unless in the writings or verbally you indicate an intent to harm oneself or someone else. At that time, a psychologist from the Department of Psychology will be notified and confidentiality will be broken in order to ensure your safety. Any new information that develops during the project will be provided if that information may affect the willingness to continue participation in the project.

Questions concerning the research, at any time during the project, should be directed to Daniel DeBrule at 266-4588 or Dr. Randy Arnau at 266-4588. This project and consent form has been reviewed by the Human Subjects Protection Review Committee, which ensures that research projects involving human subjects follow federal regulations. Any questions or concerns about rights as a research subject should be

directed to the Chair of the Institutional Review Board, The University of Southern Mississippi, Box 5147, Hattiesburg, MS 39406, (601) 266-6820.
    A copy of this form has been given to the participant.

_____   _____

Participant's Signature   Date

_____   _____

Researcher's Signature   Date

APPENDIX K
SUDS INSTRUCTIONS

S ubjective U nits of D istress S cale

We use **SUDS** to give people an idea of how upset we feel. The **SUDS** is From 0 to 10. We have given descriptions of what some of the numbers would feel like, but you are not limited to using those numbers. You can only use any number from 0 to 10. What is your **SUDS**?

10 - The most distressed you have EVER felt (total panic/ worst mood ever felt)

9

8 - Extremely distressed (furious/terrified/very depressed). Difficulty controlling emotions

7

6 - Distressed ("pissed off/scared/sad). Your emotions are strong, but under control

5

4 - Some distress (irritated/wary/"kinda bummed"). Your emotions are under control

3

2 - A little distress (mildly annoyed, a little uneasy) Your emotions are easily managed

1

0 - As relaxed as you have ever been (e.g. sitting on a beach relaxing). NO distress at all

APPENDIX L
EXPERIMENT EVALUATION FORM

The following questions pertain to the writing experiment that you completed approximately six weeks ago. Please answer these questions as honestly as possible.

	Not at all						A great deal
1. How much have you thought about the study since it ended?	1	2	3	4	5	6	7
2. How much have you talked to others about the study since it ended?	1	2	3	4	5	6	7
3. How valuable was the study to you personally?	1	2	3	4	5	6	7
4. Has writing influenced your perspective about the trauma?	1	2	3	4	5	6	7
5. Has writing influenced your emotions concerning the trauma?	1	2	3	4	5	6	7

6. How many times have you visited the health center or family doctor in the past two months?

_____

7. Do you have any additional comments concerning this study? You may want to include how writing may have helped you or hurt you, how the study could be improved, or what changes occurred due to the study.

_____
_____
_____
_____
_____
_____
_____
_____
_____

APPENDIX M
REFERRAL SERVICES

Counseling Phone Numbers

Counseling Services in Hattiesburg
Pine Belt Mental Health Resources (24 hours) 544-4641
Pine Grove Life Focus Center   288-4900

On-Campus Counseling Services

Psychology Clinic   266-4588
Counseling Clinic   266-4601
Student Services   266-4829

APPENDIX N
INSTITUTIONAL REVIEW BOARD PROTOCOL

TITLE OF STUDY: The Effect of Writing as Exposure Therapy on PTSD Symptoms

STATEMENT OF PROJECT GOALS: The primary goal of the study is to ascertain the effect that writing about a trauma has on symptoms of posttraumatic stress disorder. It is hypothesized that writing will reduce negative symptoms that follow a trauma. Specifically, symptoms are expected to decrease for those who engage in an exposure-based writing protocol compared to those who engage in the writing paradigm or a control writing exercise. In addition, process variables that may account for treatment success will also be utilized, such as subjective units of distress both within and across writing sessions, affective response to writing, and linguistic counts ascertained from writing samples.

PROTOCOL: The present investigation will utilize the writing paradigm, which has lessened trauma symptoms in several investigations (Barry & Singer, 2002; Sloan & Marx, 2004), and a variation of the writing paradigm. This paradigm consists of two or more conditions that write about a negative or trivial topic for approximately 20 minutes on four occasions. This experimental design has been found to have an effect among trauma survivors on many psychological variables, from depression (Sloan & Marx, 2004) to positive growth (Ullrich & Lutgendorf, 2002). However, recent writing studies have adjusted the writing paradigm by adding more writing time or more writing sessions, which has also lessened trauma symptoms. However, no study has compared the writing paradigm to an exposure-based variation of the writing paradigm. Thus, the present investigation will evaluate the effect of writing on three conditions: the writing paradigm, an exposure-based writing intervention, and control writing.

Overview: Approximately 100 undergraduates will be recruited for the study. A screening form will be distributed among undergraduate classes to obtain participants. Individuals will be considered for participating if they have sustained a trauma at least one month ago, and no more than seven years ago, that was personally threatening to them at the time and is still bothering them at the present time. A measure of PTSD symptoms (*Screen for Posttraumatic Stress Symptoms*, Carlson, 2001) will be utilized to include those suffering from moderate symptoms, yet exclude those suffering from minimal or severe symptoms. Those suffering from severe PTSD symptoms will be excluded from the study, and will be given a list of referrals for treatment of PTSD. Students will be contacted by phone or email if they meet the above criteria and indicate their willingness to be contacted about participation on the screening form. Each student will be given a standardized summary of the study over the phone or by email, and will be asked to participate.

Potential participants will be told that they will be required to commit to write for a total of four weekly sessions. The meetings will last for approximately forty-five to ninety minutes per session. The principal investigator will explain that the participant will be asked to complete questionnaires on the first day and six weeks after writing. They will also be told they will be writing about a specific topic that will be given to them for several minutes on each of the four days. Participants who consent to the study will be given a designated time and location to meet with principal investigator.

At the first meeting, each participant will hear a standardized greeting that includes a brief rationale of the study and a description of the participant's role. The investigator will again reiterate that the study will involve five sessions of writing and/or completing questionnaires. Participants will be told that they may be asked to write about a trauma, which may lead to some distress. The investigator will then have each participant read the informed consent form and will answer any questions before the participant signs the form. A copy of the consent form will then be given to the participant.

The investigator will then escort the consenting participant to a small, private room located within the Psychology Department at USM. To begin, each participant will develop a code name that will be used as his or her participant name throughout the study. The investigator will hand each participant a manila envelope with a sheet of paper in it. The participant will be asked to write down their name and their code on this sheet of paper in private, and then fold their line over so that the sheet will be blank. The investigator will never look at this sheet of paper throughout the study. This form will be viewed by the supervising professor if at any time in the writings the participant acknowledges a current intent to harm themselves or someone else. Next, the investigator will provide each participant with a list of phone numbers of on-campus, off-campus, and after-hour counseling services. Finally, the research assistant will ask each participant to complete several pre-test measures that will include a demographic form, the Posttraumatic Dissociation Scale (Carlson & Waelde, 2000), the Posttraumatic Checklist – Civilian Version (Weathers, Litz, Herman, Huska, & Keane, 1993), and the Impact of Events Scale-Revised (Weiss & Marmar, 1997).

Each participant will then be escorted to a private room, which will contain a computer and writing surface. Each participant will be asked if they prefer to write by hand or to type. For those who have no preference, a coin will be flipped to determine their writing format. Those who choose to write by hand will be given several writing utensils and mediums (journals, notebooks, loose leaf paper) to choose from. For those who type, each participant will be asked to write their code name on the label of the computer disk. They will be asked to open their writing instructions and begin writing or typing their essays on the computer. Participants will be randomly assigned to write about a trauma or about their plans for the day. The researcher will then shut the door for the next twenty to fifty minutes to allow the participant to write privately. After the writing time has elapsed, the research assistant will return and ask the participant to either tear out their work or save their work on a disk. Each participant will be asked to write his or her code name on the writing sample or disk, as well as on an envelope. Each sample or disk will then be sealed in the envelope and placed in a locked box. Participants will then fill out the Essay Evaluation Form, which includes questions that ask how meaningful, emotional, and personal their writing was, and provides a box that can be checked if the participant needs immediate counseling.

At the second and third meeting, the participant will again be escorted to a quiet room where they will write. The participants will be given their disk or once again choose a writing utensil and medium. The research assistant will then give the participant their sealed writing instructions to read. After writing in a private room for twenty to fifty minutes, the participant will complete the Essay Evaluation Form again, so that the participant can indicate any immediate distress or need for counseling directly after writing.

At the fourth meeting, the participant will once again write about their specified topic for twenty to fifty minutes. After the writing time has elapsed, the research assistant will again have the experimenter complete the Essay Evaluation Form.

After completing the final day of writing, the investigator will ask each participant to give an email address and/or phone numbers so that they can be contacted six weeks from their last day of writing. Participants will be told that they will receive extra credit and an entry into a cash raffle for completing follow-up measures six weeks later. The raffle will occur after data is collected and will pay 5 individuals 25 dollars. For the purpose of reimbursement from future grants, the primary researcher will obtain a signed document from each participant stating that they received a $25.00 payment for the experiment. A cash payment or meal voucher may also be given to all participants, depending on funding of the study. The researcher will also provide the same list of phone numbers of counseling services to each participant that was given at pre-test, should they feel distressed in the next six weeks, and will answer any questions, comments, or concerns. Again, should the participant appear or state that they are distressed, the appropriate protocol will be followed.

Six weeks later, participants will be contacted in order to complete several follow-up measures. These will include all of the pre-treatment dependent measures (Impact of Events Scale, the Posttraumatic Checklist – Civilian Version, and the Posttraumatic Dissociation Scale) and the Experiment Follow-up Form. After each participant has completed the writing and follow-up phases, they will be given a brief account of the study and will have the opportunity to ask questions. All participants will be asked to keep all information about the study confidential, so that no other participant will be influenced in their responses. In addition, each participant will be given the option to receive a summary of the results of the study. Those who choose this option will provide contact information and will be mailed or emailed a document containing the main results and findings of the study.

BENEFITS: Participants may become able to realize an array of positive aspects of surviving a trauma through writing. The main hypothesis of this study is that writing about a traumatic experience will decrease PTSD symptoms, thus, participants may experience improvements in frequency of nightmares, quality of sleep, arousal, and emotional range. In addition, potential benefits could be extended to those who write about a meaningless topic. Several studies have found that both the group that writes about trauma and the group that writes about a control topic can sometimes show significant improvement on the dependent measures of interest (Deters & Range, 2002). Writing paradigm studies that have been conducted at the University of Southern Mississippi have frequently been published (Kovac & Range, 1999; Kovac & Range, 2000; Range, Kovac, & Marion, 2000), and very few participants have claimed that they required immediate counseling during eight writing paradigm studies that have been conducted at the University of Southern Mississippi. Furthermore, many participants report that they have benefited in some way from writing about their trauma, and that they found the experiment to be a worthwhile exercise. Each participant will also have the potential benefit of earning twenty-five dollars if they complete the study and win the cash raffle.

RISKS AND PROCEDURES TO MINIMIZE RISKS:

Three methodological aspects of the present study will minimize risk of harm to participants.One, the primary investigator, a Masters-level clinical psychology graduate student, will read all essays within 24 hours of completion to assess current intent to harm self or someone else throughout the study. Should any essay describe an intention of harming oneself or others, the principal investigator will consult the supervising professor so that the supervisor can match the name to the code and take appropriate action (i.e. phone contact, referral). Two, each participant will be given the opportunity to check a box on the Essay Evaluation Form to indicate if they would like immediate counseling. Three, the investigator will also provide each participant with a list of phone numbers of on-campus, off-campus, and after-hour counseling services.

At all stages of the study, the principal investigator and the research assistant will assess whether a participant appears distressed or upset in any way before or after writing. Also, writing samples will be thoroughly read within 24 hours of completion for any mention of suicide, violence, or distress. In addition, participants will be given the opportunity to check a box on the Essay Evaluation Form indicating they need immediate counseling. A detailed protocol was developed to assess and manage distress and/or suicidality, which rarely occurs during writing interventions. This protocol will be followed should a participant present with acute distress or potential of harm. All participants will also be given phone numbers to call in case they have any mental health concern or distress. Although the essays and dependent measures will be coded throughout the study, if at any time a participant indicates in their writing or verbally a current intent to harm themselves or others, confidentiality will be broken. Participants that check a box indicating that they would like to speak to a mental health professional will be escorted to the USM Counseling Center. Participants will also receive this service if they mention harm to self or others verbally or in writing. Participants will be informed that fees may be involved for such services, for which they are responsible.

Participants will be advised that their participation in this study is voluntary. They will be advised that they may withdraw from being a research participant at any time during the study. If they withdraw from this study voluntarily, participants will be advised that they will receive course credit for the portions of the research that they have completed. All data, including computer disks, and any hand written essays will be stored in a locked office and only the investigator and Dr. Arnau will have access to the writing samples. All of the data will be destroyed after five years have passed since the beginning of the study.

Appendix O
OFFICIAL APPROVAL FORM FROM INSTITUTIONAL REVIEW BOARD

1

25062005

Protocol # _____ (office use only)
HUMAN SUBJECTS REVIEW FORM
UNIVERSITY OF SOUTHERN MISSISSIPPI
(Submit this form in duplicate)

Name: <u>Daniel S. DeBrule</u>   Phone: <u>4588</u> or <u>582-3771</u>

Mailing Address: <u>133 Cooper St. Hattiesburg, MS 39401</u>
(address to receive information regarding this application)

College/Division: <u>Education and Psychology</u>   Dept: <u>Psychology</u>

Department Box # <u>5025</u>   Phone: <u>4177</u>

Proposed Project Dates: From: <u>1-10-05</u>   To: <u>6-15-06</u>
(specific month, day and year of the beginning and ending dates of full project, not just data collection)

Title: The Effect of Writing as Exposure Therapy on PTSD Symptoms

Funding Agencies or Research Sponsors: <u>N/A</u>

Grant Number (when applicable): <u>N/A</u>

_____ New Project

___X___ Dissertation or Thesis

_____ Renewal or Continuation: Protocol #

_____ Change in Previously Approved Project: Protocol #

Principal Investigator _____ Date **5/16/05**

Advisor _____ Date 6/16/05

Department Chair _____ Date 6/16/05

RECOMMENDATION OF HSPRC MEMBER

_____ Category I, Exempt under Subpart A, Section 46.101 ( ) ( ), 45CFR46.

___X___ Category II, Expedited Review, Subpart A, Section 46.110 and Subparagraph (b).

_____ Category III, Full Committee Review. The applicant has been requested to provide the Office of Research and Sponsored Programs (ORSP) with twelve (12) additional copies of the application.

_____
HSPRC College/Division Member   Date 7-7-05

_____
HSPRC Chair   Date 7-15-05

APPENDIX P
OFFICIAL LETTER OF APPROVAL FROM INSTITUTIONAL REVIEW BOARD

The University of
Southern Mississippi

Institutional Review Board

11B College Drive #5147
Hattiesburg, MS 39406-0001
Tel: 601.266.6820
Fax: 601.266.5509
www.usm.edu/irb

HUMAN SUBJECTS PROTECTION REVIEW COMMITTEE
NOTICE OF COMMITTEE ACTION

The project has been reviewed by The University of Southern Mississippi Human Subjects Protection Review Committee in accordance with Federal Drug Administration regulations (21 CFR 26, 111), Department of Health and Human Services (45 CFR Part 46), and university guidelines to ensure adherence to the following criteria:

- The risks to subjects are minimized.
- The risks to subjects are reasonable in relation to the anticipated benefits.
- The selection of subjects is equitable.
- Informed consent is adequate and appropriately documented.
- Where appropriate, the research plan makes adequate provisions for monitoring the data collected to ensure the safety of the subjects.
- Where appropriate, there are adequate provisions to protect the privacy of subjects and to maintain the confidentiality of all data.
- Appropriate additional safeguards have been included to protect vulnerable subjects.
- Any unanticipated, serious, or continuing problems encountered regarding risks to subjects must be reported immediately, but not later than 10 days following the event. This should be reported to the IRB Office via the "Adverse Effect Report Form".
- If approved, the maximum period of approval is limited to twelve months. Projects that exceed this period must submit an application for renewal or continuation.

PROTOCOL NUMBER: 25062005
PROJECT TITLE: **The Effect of Writing as Exposure Therapy on PTSD Symptoms**
PROPOSED PROJECT DATES: **01/10/05 to 06/15/06**
PROJECT TYPE: **Dissertation or Thesis**
PRINCIPAL INVESTIGATORS: Daniel S. DeBrule
COLLEGE/DIVISION: **College of Education & Psycholgoy**
DEPARTMENT: **Psychology**
FUNDING AGENCY: **N/A**
HSPRC COMMITTEE ACTION: **Expedited Review Approval**
PERIOD OF APPROVAL: **07/13/05 to 07/12/06**

Lawrence A. Hosman, Ph.D.
HSPRC Chair

7-15-05
Date

Agargun, M. Y., Kara, H., Ozer, O. A., Slevi, Y., Kiran, U., & Ozer, B. (2003). Clinical importance of nightmare disorder in patients with dissociative disorders. *Psychiatry and Neurosciences, 57,* 575-579.

American Psychiatric Association. (2000) *Diagnostic and statistical manual of mental disorders.* 4th ed. Washington, D. C.: American Psychiatric Association.

Antal, H.A., & Range, L. M. (2005). Psychological impact of writing about abuse or positive experiences. *Violence and Victims, 20,* 717-728.

Astin, M. C., & Rothbaum, B. O. (2000). Exposure therapy for the treatment of Posttraumatic Stress Disorder. *Clinical Quarterly of the National Center for PTSD, 9,* 49-54.

Asukai, N., Kato, H., Kawamura, N., Kim, Y., Yamamoto, K., Kishimoto, J., Miyake, Y., et al. (2002). Reliability and validity of the Japanese-language version of the Impact of Event Scale-revised (IES-R-J). *Journal of Nervous and Mental Disease, 190,* 175-182.

Baguena, M., Belena, A., Armelia, D., Roldan, C., & Reig, R. (2001). Psychometric properties of the Spanish version of the Impact of Events Scale-Revised. *Analisis y Modification de Conducta, 27,* 581-604.

Balkie, K. A. (2008). Who does expressive writing work for? Examination of alexythymia, splitting, and repressive coping style as moderators of the expressive writing paradigm. *British Journal of Health Psychology, 13,* 61-66.

Barry, L. M., & Singer, G. H. (2001). Reducing maternal psychological distress after the

NICU experience through journal writing. *Journal of Early Intervention, 24,* 287-297.

Batten, S. V., Follette, V. M., Rasmussen Hall, M. L., & Palm, K. M. (2002). Physical and psychological effects of written disclosure among sexual abuse survivors. *Behavior Therapy, 33,* 107-122.

Beven, J. L., Avila, L. A., Blake, E. S., Brown, D. P., Franklin, J. L., Knabb, R. D., Pasch, R. J., et al. (2008). Atlantic hurricane season of 2005. *Monthly Weather Review, 136,* 1109-1173.

Blake, D. D., Weathers, F. W., Nagy, L. M. Kaloupek, D. G., Gusman, F. D., Cahrney, D. S., & Keane, T. M. (1995). The Development of a clinician administered PTSD Scale. *Journal of Traumatic Stress, 8,* 75-90.

Blanchard, E. B., Jones-Alexander, J., Buckley, T. C., Forneris, C. A. (1996). Psychometric properties of the PTSD checklist. *Behavior Research and Therapy, 34,* 669-673.

Bonanno, G. A. (2004). Loss, trauma, and human resilience: Have we underestimated the human capacity to thrive after extremely aversive events? *American Psychologist, 59,* 20-28.

Brom, D., Kleber, R. J., & Defares, P. B. (1989). Brief psychotherapy for posttraumatic stress disorders. *Journal of Consulting and Clinical Psychology, 57,* 607-612.

Brown, E. J., & Heimberg, R. G. (2001). Effects of writing about rape: Evaluating Pennebaker's writing paradigm with a severe trauma. *Journal of Traumatic Stress, 14,* 781-790.

Brunet, A. St. Hilaire, A., Jehel, L., & King, S. (2003). Validation of a French version of the Impact of Events Scale-Revised. *Canadian Journal of Psychiatry, 48,* 56-61.

Carlson, E. B. (2001). Psychometric study of a brief screen for PTSD: Assessing the Impact of Multiple Traumatic Events. *Assessment, 8,* 431-441.

Carlson, E. B., & Dutton, M. A. (2003). Assessing experiences and responses of crime victims. *Journal of Traumatic Events, 16,* 133-148.

Carlson, E. B., & Dalenberg, C. (2000). A conceptual framework for the impact of traumatic experiences *Trauma, Violence, and Abuse, 1,* 4-28.

Carlson, E. B., & Waelde, L. W. (2000, November). Preliminary psychometric properties of the Posttraumatic Dissociation Scale. Presented at the annual meeting of the International Society for Traumatic Stress Studies. San Antonio, TX.

Carroll, E. M., & Foy, D. W. (1992). Assessment and treatment of combat-related Posttraumatic Stress Disorder in a medical setting. In D. W. Foy (Ed.). *Treating PTSD: Cognitive behavioral strategies.* Guilford Press: New York, NY.

Cooper, N. A., & Clum, G. A. (1989). Imaginal flooding as a supplementary treatment for PTSD in combat veterans: A controlled study. *Behavior Therapy, 3,* 381-391.

Creamer, M., Bell, R., & Failla, S. (2003). Psychometric properties of the Impact of Events Scale-Revised. *Behavior Research & Therapy, 41,* 1489-1496.

Creamer, M., Burgess, P., & Pattison, P. (1992). Reaction to trauma: A cognitive processing model. *Journal of Abnormal Psychology, 101 (3),* 452-459.

Davidson, J. R., Hughes, D., Blazer, D. G. Posttraumatic stress disorder in the community: An epidemiological study. *Psychological Medicine, 21,* 713-721.

DeBrule, D. S., & Range, L. M. (2005, March). Does writing about a trauma enhance posttraumatic growth? Poster session presented at the annual meeting of the Southeastern Psychological Association.

Deters, P. B. & Range, L. M. (2003). Does writing reduce Posttraumatic Stress Disorder symptoms? *Violence & Victims, 18*, 569-580.

Donnelly, D., & Murray, E. (1991). Cognitive and emotional changes in written essays and therapy interviews. *Journal of Social and Clinical Psychology, 10*, 334-350.

Everly, G. S., & Lating, J. M. (1995). *Psychotraumatology: Key papers and core concepts in post-traumatic stress.* New York: Plenum Press.

Foa, E. B., & Kozak, M. J. (1986). Emotional processing of fear: Exposure to corrective information. *Psychological Bulletin, 99*, 20-35.

Foa, E. B., & Meadows, E. A. (1997). Psychosocial treatments for Posttraumatic Stress Disorder: A critical review. *Annual Review of Psychology, 48*, 449-480.

Foa, E. B., Rothbaum, B. O., Riggs, D., & Murdock, T. (1991). Treatment of posttraumatic stress disorder in rape victims: A comparison between cognitive-behavioral procedures and counseling. *Journal of Consulting and Clinical Psychology, 59*, 715-723.

Fontana A., & Rosenheck R. (1998). Psychological benefits and liabilities of traumatic exposure in the war zone. *Journal of Traumatic Stress, 12*, 111-126.

Francis, M. E. & Pennebaker, J. W. (1992). Putting stress into words: The impact of writing on physiological., absentee, and self-reported emotional well-being measures. *American Journal of Health Promotion, 6*, 280-287.

Galea, S., Brewin, C. R., Gruber, M., Jones, R. T., King, D. W., McNally, R. J., Ursano, R. J. et al. (2007). Exposure to hurricane-related stressors and mental illness after Hurricane Katrina. *Archives of General Psychiatry, 64,* 1427-1424.

Gidron, Y., Peri, T., Connolly, J. F., & Shalev, A. Y. (1996). Written disclosure in posttraumatic stress disorder: Is it beneficial for the patient? *Journal of Nervous and Mental Disease, 184,* 505-507.

Greenberg, M. A. & Stone A. A. (1992). Emotional disclosure about traumas and its relation to health: Effects of previous disclosure and trauma severity. *Journal of Personality and Social Psychology, 63,* 75-84.

Guastella, A. J., & Dadds, M. R. (2006). Cognitive-behavioral models of emotional writing: A validation study. *Cognitive Therapy & Research, 30,* 397-414.

Harris, A. H. (2006). Does expressive writing reduce health care utilization? *Journal of Consulting and Clinical Psychology, 74,* 243-252.

Horowitz, M., Wilner, N., & Alvarez, W. (1979). Impact of Events Scale: A measure of subjective stress. *Psychosomatic Medicine, 41,* 209-218.

Jaycox, L. H., Foa, E. B., & Morral, A. R. (1998). Influence of emotional engagement and habituation on exposure therapy for PTSD. *Journal of Consulting and Clinical Psychology, 66,* 185-193.

Janoff-Bulman, R. (1992). *Shattered assumptions.* New York: The Free Press.

Keane, T. M. Fairbank, J. A., Caddell, J. M., Zimering, R. T. (1989) Implosive (flooding) therapy reduces symptoms of PTSD in Vietnam combat veterans. *Behavior Therapy, 20,* 245-260.

Kessler, R., Sonnega, A., Bromet, E. & Nelson, C. B. (1995). Posttraumatic Stress
Disorder in the National Comorbidity Survey. *Archives of General Psychiatry, 52,*
1048-1060.

Kilpatrick, D. G., Veronen, L. J., Resick, P. A. (1982). Psychological sequelae to rape:
Assessment and treatment strategies. In D. M. Dolays, & R. L. Meredith, R. L.
(Eds.) *Behavioral medicine: Assessment and treatment strategies.* Plenum Press:
New York.

King, C. A. (2004). A promising psychosocial intervention: Next steps include systematic
study and creative extension. *Clinical Psychology: Science and Practice, 11,*
143-146.

Klein, K., & Boals, A. (2001). Expressive writing can increase working memory
capacity. *Journal of Experimental Psychology, 130,* 520-533.

Kloss, J. D., & Lisman, S. A. (2002). An exposure-based examination of the effects of
written emotional disclosure. *British Journal of Health Psychology, 7,* 31-46.

Kovac, S.H., & Range, L.M. (1999). Does writing about suicidal thoughts and feelings
reduce them? *Archives of Suicide Research, 3,* 122-128.

Kovac, S.H., & Range, L.M. (2000). Writing projects: Lessening undergraduates' unique
suicidal bereavement. *Suicide and Life-Threatening Behavior, 30,* 50-60.

Kring, A. M., Davison, G. C., Neale, J. M., & Johnson, S. L. (2007). *Abnormal
Psychology.* San Francisco, CA: Wiley & Sons.

Lang, A. J., Lafeyye, C., Satz, L.E., Dresselhaus, T. R., & Stein, M. B. (2003).
Sensitivity and Specificity of the PTSD Checklist in Detecting PTSD in female

veterans in primary care. *Journal of Traumatic Stress, 16,* 257-264.

Lango-Marsh, L., & Spates, C. R. (2002). The effects of writing therapy in comparison to

EMD/R on traumatic stress. *Professional Psychology: Research & Practice, 33,*

581-586.

Lepore, S. A. (1997). Expressive writing moderates the relation between intrusive

thoughts and depressive symptoms. *Journal of Personality and Social*

Psychology, 73, 1030-1037.

Lindy, J. D., Green, B. L., Grace, M., & Titchener, J. (1983). Psychotherapy with

survivors of the Beverly Hills Supper Club Fire. *American Journal of*

Psychotherapy, 4, 593-610.

Littrell, J. (1999). Is the reexperience of painful emotion therapeutic? *Clinical*

Psychology Review, 18, 71-102.

Lyons, J. A., & Keane, T. M. (1989). Implosive therapy for the treatment of combat-

related PTSD. *Journal of Traumatic Stress, 2,* 137-152.

Mann, T. (2001). Effects of future writing and optimism on health behaviors. *Annals of*

Behavioral Medicine, 23, 26-33.

Marx, B. A., & Sloan, D. M. (2005). Peritraumatic dissociation and experiential

avoidance as predictors of posttraumatic stress symptomology. *Behavior*

Research & Therapy, 43, 569-583.

McDonald, A. S. (1997). Factor structure of the Impact of Events Scale in a non-clinical

sample. *Personality and Individual Differences, 23,* 419-424.

Meadows, E. A., & Foa, E. B. (1998). Intrusion, arousal, and avoidance: Sexual trauma survivors. In: V. M. Follette, & J. I. Ruzek (Eds.), *Cognitive-behavioral therapies for trauma* (pp. 100-123). New York, NY: Guilford Press.

Mowrer, O. H. (1960). Two-factor learning theory: Versions one and two. In: O. H. Mowrer, *Learning Theory and Behavior*. Hoboken, NJ: John Wiley and Sons.

Nolen-Hoeksema, S., & Morrow, J. (1991). A prospective study of depression and posttraumatic stress symptoms after a natural disaster. *Journal of Personality and Social Psychology, 61,* 115-121.

Paez, D., Velasco, C., & Gonzales, J. L. (1999). Expressive writing and the role of alexithymia as a dispositional deficit in self-disclosure and psychological health. *Journal of Personality and Social Psychology, 77,* 630-641.

Pennebaker, J. W. (2004). *Writing to heal: A guided journal for recovering from trauma and emotional upheaval*. Oakland, CA: New Harbinger Publications.

Pennebaker, J. W. (1989). Confession, inhibition, and disease. In L. Berkowitz (Ed.), *Advances in experimental social psychology* (Vol. 22, pp. 211-244). New York: Academic Press.

Pennebaker, J. W., & Beall, S. K. (1986). Confronting a traumatic event: Toward an understanding of inhibition and disease. *Journal of Abnormal Psychology, 95,* 274-281.

Pennebaker, J. W., & Francis, M. (1996). Cognitive, emotional, and language processes in disclosure. *Cognition and Emotion, 10,* 601-626.

Pennebaker, J. W., Kiecolt-Glaser, J. K., & Glaser, R. (1996). Disclosure of traumas and immune function: Health implications for psychotherapy. *Journal of Consulting and Clinical Psychology, 56,* 239-245.

Pennebaker, J.W., Francis, M.E., & Booth, R.J. (2001). *Linguistic Inquiry and Word Count (LIWC): A Computerized Text Analysis Program.* Mahwah NJ: Earlbaum Publishers.

Petrie, K., Booth, R., & Pennebaker, J. (1998). The immunological effects of thought suppression. *Journal of Personality and Social Psychology, 75,* 1264-1272.

Range, L.M., Kovac, S. H., & Marion, M.S. (2000). Does writing about the bereavement lessen grief following sudden, unintentional death? *Death Studies, 2,* 115-134.

Resick, P. A., Galovski, T. E., Uhlmansiek, M. O., Shcer, C. D., Clum, G. A., & Young-Xu, Y. (2008). A randomized clinical trial to dismantle components of cognitive processing therapy for posttraumatic stress disorder in female victims of interpersonal violence. *Journal of Consulting and Clinical Psychology, 76,* 243-258.

Resick, P. A., Nishith, P., Weaver, T. L., Astin, M. C., & Feuer, C. A. (2002). A comparison of cognitive-processing therapy and a waiting condition for the treatment of chronic posttraumatic stress disorder in female rape victims. *Journal of Consulting and Clinical Psychology, 70,* 867-879.

Resick, P. A., & Schnicke, M. K. (1992a). Cognitive Processing Therapy for rape victims: A treatment manual. Sagebrush Publications: Thousand Oaks, CA.

Resick, P. A., & Schnicke, M. K. (1992b). Cognitive Processing Therapy for sexual assault victims. *Journal of Consulting and Clinical Psychology, 60,* 748-756.

Richards, J. M., Beal, W. E., Seagal, J. D., & Pennebaker, J. W. (2000). Effects of disclosure of traumatic events on illness behavior among psychiatric prison inmates. *Journal of Abnormal Psychology, 109,* 156-160.

Rogers, L. J., Wilson, K. G., Gohm, C. L., & Merwin, G. M. (2007). Written disclosure revisited: the effects of cold versus warm experimenters. *Journal of Social and Clinical Psychology, 26,* 556-574.

Rothbaum, B. O., Meadows, E. A., & Resick P. (2000) Cognitive behavioral treatments for PTSD. In: E. B. Foa & T. M. Keane. *Effective treatments for PTSD.* Guilford: New York.

Ruggiero, K. J., Del Ben, K., Scotti, J. R., & Rabalais, A. E. (2003). Psychometric Properties of the PTSD Checklist – Civilian Version. *Journal of Traumatic Stress, 16,* 495-502.

Schell, T. L., Marshall, G. N., & Jaycox, L. H. (2004). All symptoms are not created equal: The prominent role of hyperarousal in the natural course of posttraumatic psychological distress. *Journal of Abnormal Psychology, 113,* 189-197.

Schoutrop, M. J. A., Lange, A. Hanewald, G., Davidovich, U., & Salomon, H. (2002). Structured writing and processing major stressful events: A controlled trial. *Psychotherapy and Psychosomatics, 71,* 151-157.

Scott, J., Harrington, J., House, R., & Ferrier, I. (1999). Written disclosure in posttraumatic stress disorder: Is it beneficial for the patient? *Journal of Nervous and Mental Disease, 184,* 505-507.

Shalev, A. Y., Bonne, O. & Eth, S. (1996). Treatment of Posttraumatic Stress Disorder: A review. *Psychosomatic Medicine, 58,* 165-182.

Sloan, D. M., & Marx, B. P. (2004). A closer examination of the structured written disclosure procedure. *Journal of Consulting and Clinical Psychology, 72,* 165-175.

Sloan, D. M., & Marx, B. P., & Epstein, E. M. (2005). Further examination of the exposure model underlying the efficacy of written emotional disclosure. *Journal of Consulting and Clinical Psychology, 73,* 549-554.

Sloan, D. M., Marx, B. P., Epstein, E. M., & Lexington, J. M. (2007). Does altering the writing instructions influence outcome associated with written disclosure? *Behavior Therapy, 38,* 155-168.

Smyth, J. M. (1998). Written emotional expression: Effect sizes, outcome types, and moderating variables. *Journal of Consulting and Clinical Psychology, 66,* 174-184.

Smyth, J. M., Hockemeyer, J. H., Anderson, C. A., Strandberg, K., Koch, M., O'Neill, H. K., & McCammon, S. (2002). Structured writing about a natural disaster buffers the effect of intrusive thoughts on negative affect and physical symptoms. *Australasian Journal of Disaster and Trauma Studies, (1),* 1-11.

Smyth, J. M., Stone, A., Hurewitz, A., & Kaell, A. (2000). Effects of writing about stressful experiences on symptom reduction in patients with asthma or rheumatoid arthritis. *Journal of the American Medical Association, 281,* 1304-1309.

Smyth, J. M., True, N., & Souto, J. (2001). Effects of writing about traumatic experiences: The necessity for narrative structuring. *Journal of Social & Clinical Psychology, 20,* 161-172.

Ullrich, P. M., & Lutgendorf, S. K. (2002). Journaling about stressful events: Effects of cognitive processing and emotional expression. *Annals of Behavioral Medicine, 24 (3)*, 244-250.

Weathers, F., Litz, B., Herman, D., Huska, J., & Keane, T. (October, 1993). The PTSD Checklist (PCL): Reliability, Validity, and Diagnostic Utility. Paper presented at the Annual Convention of the International Society of Traumatic Stress Studies. San Antonio, TX.

Weiss, D. S., & Marmar, C. R. (1996). The Impact of Events Scale – Revised. In J. Wilson & T. M. Keane (Eds.), *Assessing psychological trauma & PTSD*. New York: Guilford Press.

Wolpe, J. (1973). *The practice of behavior therapy*. New York: Pergamon Press.

Yehuda, R. (2002). Current status of cortisol findings in post-traumatic stress disorder. *Psychiatric Clinics of North America, 25*, 341-368.

Yehuda, R., Marshall, R., Penkower, A., & Wong, C. M. (2002). Phamacological treatments for posttraumatic stress disorder. In: P. E. Nathan. *A Guide to Treatments that Work*. Oxford: New York.